TWO GUYS READ THE BOX SCORES

Steve Chandler & Terrence N. Hill

Conversations on Baseball and Other Metaphysical Wonders

Robert D. Reed Publishers   •   Bandon, OR

Robert D. Reed Publishers
P.O. Box 1992
Bandon, OR 97411
Phone: 541-347-9882; Fax: -9883
E-mail: 4bobreed@msn.com
Website: www.rdrpublishers.com

Editor: Kathy Chandler
Cover photograph is by Ryan Hoffman -
    http://www.ryanhoffmanphoto.com/
Front cover design by Angela Hardison / SeeSaw Designs
Back cover photo copyright Kathy Chandler
Typesetter: Debby Gwaltney

Mixed Sources
Product group from well-managed forests and other controlled sources
www.fsc.org Cert no. SW-COC-002283
© 1996 Forest Stewardship Council

ISBN: 978-1-934759-47-9
ISBN 10: 1-934759-47-3

Library of Congress Number: 2010902007

Manufactured, Typeset, and Printed in the United States of America

To Terry Hill

(Who, although he is the co-author of this book,
deserves the dedication, for reasons you shall see.)

Introduction

We were the real boys of summer

The year was 1955 and it was springtime in Birmingham, Michigan, a great time and place to be alive if you were eleven years old as we were.

Each morning I read my favorite sportswriter Joe Falls as he reported on developments for the Tigers' spring training in Florida. I was wistful, dreamy, and lazy.

That would soon change.

Because that was the year I met another eleven-year-old who would become my lifelong friend and who would immediately change my life for the better. He was tall and wiry, had red hair and freckles, and looked like he walked right out of a Norman Rockwell painting.

This person would later become the author, playwright, advertising creative director, world traveler, horse racing aficionado, country folk singer Terrence N. Hill, but back then he was just Terry.

Before I met him I had been a young baseball fan in a rather relaxed, distant way. I read the sports pages and listened to games on the radio. In my cocoon of passivity. But Terry is not a passive person. Neither does he enjoy passivity in others. (Try vacationing with him. You'll need to take a vacation *after* the vacation to recover.)

Terry engages life full-out. So it wasn't long before he had me following baseball at deeper levels than most boys ever do. And he also convinced me to try out for Little League and play the game, too.

Ralph Waldo Emerson said, "A true friend is someone who will make us do what we can."

That was Terry.

About a year after befriending him I was sitting on the floor of my bedroom with baseball cards neatly aligned next to a stenographer's notebook as I rolled dice to see what the next player would do at bat. I'd then record the result on the pad, and after a while there were huge stacks of pads piled high with statistics. Terry and I had invented a game, a precursor to today's fantasy leagues: we simply called it "Leagues."

Like baseball-addicted mad scientists we'd play, sometimes ten hours straight, long into the night, and then rush to each other's houses the next day to report the results. We owned and memorized every baseball card of every player in major league baseball, and our knowledge of the sport's trivia would make Bill James (later to become baseball's greatest statistician) look woefully uninformed.

To speed up the accumulation of our fantasy statistics, we taught ourselves to use an abacus. We later learned to use a slide rule, marvelous for quickly calculating batting averages and ERAs.

And out in the yard we also played. Hours on end! We cut golf balls open to get at the hard, bouncy little ball in the middle and then used that ball to throw off various walls and garage doors. We also played catch, and fungo, and soon were playing on the same team, the Wildcats, in Little League. Terry was our shortstop and I played third base. We were champions. Terry was the sparkplug.

We were so into baseball that the real world had become a mere alternative universe. We did follow real sports, but they were never quite as exciting as the leagues we ourselves created and wrote about.

Back then, living outside Detroit, it was safe for two boys to take a bus to Briggs Stadium downtown to watch our Tiger heroes: Ray Boone, who led the league in runs batted in during 1955; Al Kaline, who was the league's best hitter (.340); and Harvey Kuenn, who captained the team and led the league in doubles. Our Tigers scored more runs than any team in the American League although the Yankees (with Mickey Mantle and his unbeatable rat pack) ran away with the pennant.

That was a long time ago, though, no? And, so, here we are fifty-four years later. What's changed? Almost nothing! So we wrote this book about baseball.

This was a year Dickens would have liked because Terry and I followed the best of teams and the worst of teams. Terry, who has long been a New Yorker, got to follow his Yankees all the way to the World Championship. (Sorry for spoiling the ending.)

I, myself, followed my own hometown Arizona Diamondbacks.

Dysfunction in uniform.

As a part of this book's research we decided to spend a week together in New York, going to games and visiting the Baseball Hall of Fame in Cooperstown. Terry also spent a weekend in Phoenix to see my team play. The wonderful thing about that was that we had as much fun this time around as we used to have when we both lived on Buckingham Road in 1955, just a few houses apart from each other.

There is no real rhyme or reason to this book. No attempt to chronicle a season comprehensively. It's really about two fans having fun following baseball and writing to each other about it.

Terry did a better job telling the story of the Yankees season, and I'm glad he did, because everybody loves a winner. (Damn Yankees!) I, on the other hand, felt I had an obligation to the readers not to make them depressed ... so I tried to write as little about the Diamondbacks as I could.

This is our fourth book together. We started on a whim. We were initially trying to get into the Guinness World Records book as the first people to ever read *Moby Dick* all the way through. We decided to make our correspondence about that reading experience into a book, and to our surprise a lot of people really enjoyed it, and are still buying copies today.

So we fantasized that we were now pressured to write more books together. Terry had been mailing me his favorite obituaries for decades so we hit upon *Two Guys Read the Obituaries* as a fun sequel. To our fresh surprise, people bought that one, too. Not in Harry Potter numbers, but enough books were sold to forge ahead with our third book, *Two Guys Read Jane Austen*.

That one sold more copies than the first two combined! Other authors were now becoming envious. It is said that at one publishing convention a long line of writers paraded outside the convention hall carrying signs that said: "Break up the Two Guys!"

But they would not stop writing.

One of the Austen books that we wrote about was *Mansfield Park,* the dust jacket of which describes Jane's mission as an author. It says it was her mission to "...express her faith in a social order that combats chaos through civil grace, decency and wit."

That's baseball's mission, too. In these chaotic times, there is always baseball. It is just a game. But it can restore us to sanity.

We talk in this book a lot about the great baseball player Ichiro. Yes, he goes by one name and this book explains why. Although there's another explanation, too. He is as masterful at his art as other one-name people like Picasso or Sting or Elvis are at theirs.

So I'm going to finish this by telling you something Ichiro said once. And I hope I can get this in because sometimes Terry likes to edit my writing out when I go too far in the direction of my passion for personal growth and the psychology of achievement.

At the prospect of first facing Red Sox pitcher and fellow countryman Daisuke Matsuzaka, Ichiro said, "I hope he arouses the fire that's dormant in the innermost recesses of my soul. I plan to face him with the zeal of a challenger."

Boy do I ever love that quote. The fire in my soul. The zeal of a challenger. I love his quote almost as much as I love baseball itself. And I have Terry to thank for that.

So onward into this season. I hope you feel our love of baseball in all of these pages.

Steve Chandler
Phoenix, Arizona
January, 2010

1 March 2009
San Miguel de Allende, Mexico

Dear Steve,

I'd been so looking forward to writing a baseball book with you. Especially this year when it's clear to every intelligent fan that the Yankees are going home with World Series rings.

I mean with the best starting pitching rotation money can buy, how can they miss?

Look at it this way: Sabathia, Wong, Pettitte, Chamberlain and Burnett; each pretty much a cinch to win 20. Well there's the pennant right there. After that, why even bother to have the Playoffs and the World Series? I actually *know* why they bother, because it's too much money to pass up. The actual outcome itself isn't in doubt.

Of course, this is how I've felt every spring since about 1953. I've always felt my team has a great shot at going all the way – even when it's clear they don't. I don't worry about this much though, because it's a blind spot I believe I share with every baseball fan. (For instance, you're probably thinking the Diamondbacks have a shot. They don't, but right now you're thinking if a few players step up their game a bit, this could be their year.)

Hope springs eternal, they say. But for baseball fans, hope is eternal in the spring. That's why I love the arrival of spring training so much. Or did ... until *Sports Illustrated* reveals that Alex Rodriguez took steroids 2001 to 2003.

I gotta say it put a serious damper on my excitement of the upcoming season ... and on my anticipation of writing this book.

Say it ain't so, Alex.

In New York, just before coming down here for the winter, Miranda and I saw a play on Broadway called "Back Back Back." It was about baseball, and the title echoes the broadcast announcer's traditional call on a long fly ball. ("There's a deep fly ball to left! Matsui goes back, back, back ...") But the title has a double meaning because as the play opens in the locker room of an unnamed major league team in Oakland, one of the players is on the verge of becoming the third straight Rookie of the Year winner from this team.

In other words, Oakland is about to win the Rookie Award ... *back to back to back.*

The entire play has only these three characters and it follows their careers and lives over the next 20–25 years. The printed program for the play made a point of saying that this was entirely a work of fiction and, in fact, none of the characters' names are recognizable major league players. However, about a third of the way through the play, you realize that this disclaimer is merely legally protective bullshit.

For instance, the Oakland manager's name is "Tony." The first Rookie of the Year is a totally self-absorbed outfielder of Cuban descent from Miami. He is wildly pumped on steroids and shares them with the second rookie, a power-hitting first baseman. Tony, the manager, later moves to manage a team in St. Louis and soon brings his old first baseman with him. The first baseman proceeds to break the single-season home run record and looks like a cinch for the Hall of Fame.

The steroid scandal then breaks, in part because the Cuban rookie writes a tell-all book. Both the first and the second rookies are called to testify before Congress and the home run champ comes across as an evasive dissembler at the hearing and now it looks as if he'll never make it into the Hall. That's basically the plot of the play.

Does any of that sound familiar to you? Because, by coincidence, it happens that in 1986, '87 and '88, players from the Oakland Athletics (then managed by "Tony" La Russa) won the Rookie of the Year Award back to back to back. Full marks for identifying José Canseco and Mark McGwire, plus a huge bonus if you got Walt Weiss.

I must say, the play was very good even if you didn't have all the back story logged in your memory. It was played as a modern day tragedy. And the three players, who started their careers with such bright promise, wind up with either their reputations blackened (Canseco and McGwire) or totally disillusioned (Weiss.) But, of course, the play also makes the point that it is the game of baseball that suffered the real tragedy.

Do you think that's true? If you're being totally rational, you have to admit that the "game" itself is pretty much unchanged: it's still 90 feet to first base, 60 feet six inches from the pitcher's mound to the plate, right?

But, of course, that's ridiculous. The game is so much more than a set of rules. The game is the players who've played it, the fields they've played on, the fans who've watched it, the writers who've written about it; it's history, statistics, folklore, memories and so much more. And yes, for me, a lot of that has been badly damaged by steroids.

Consider Ryan Howard. The man hit 48 home runs for the Phillies last year, 8 more than anybody else in the majors. But he looks like a banjo hitter compared to Barry Bonds' 73 in 2001. So seriously, what do we do with all those records from the 1990s and early 2000s? Just throw them out and pretend they didn't happen, like the 1994 World Series?

Frankly, I'm mad as Hell and I'm not going to take it anymore … until the new season starts.

terry.

4 March 2009 – Gilbert, Arizona

Dear Terry,

Baseball is all you need to know if you want to study life. It's the perfect metaphor.

I refer, of course, to your Yankees and the team they have purchased this year. Here's the life lesson we want to learn: can one throw huge amounts of money at a problem and solve it that way? We can track the car companies in our beloved major league hometown of Detroit to answer that question, or we can follow your Yankees.

Remember when you and I took English class together in high school? We had Miss Allen, and every week we had new vocabulary words to learn. What seemed tedious to us then was amazingly unforgettable in retrospect. One of her words ... do you remember? ...was "impecunious." Meaning not pecunious. Which means unable to afford things. Like a starting pitching staff of 20-game winners. Like your team has.

My team here in this town is impecunious! So we pin some of our hopes on a young third baseman who led the league in errors *and* strikeouts last year. I'm all for learning to fail and move on, but that's a nightmare version of that.

Our manager's nickname, however, is "The Mad Scientist." So that makes me believe that he might be a kind of baseball alchemist, and make a pennant contender out of this group. I know I must sound crazy, but I honestly think these Diamondbacks have a chance this year to go all the way.

Tell me because I know you'll know. You were always more of a numbers guy than I was. Did A-Rod's steroid use really help him? Did it truly give him an unfair advantage? Haven't his numbers been as good without them? His head didn't get huge (physically, anyway) like Barry Bonds' head did. His numbers didn't inflate grotesquely like McGwire's and Bonds' and Sosa's versus their non-drug days. So it's harder for me to be upset.

It seems like it wasn't that big a deal for him. It was almost as if the drugs had no real power to improve what his body could already do. Am I wrong?

Were there side effects I'm unaware of? Maybe so, because I heard he left his wife last year and started dating Madonna. Would someone with a healthy mind and body even consider that?

For about a year I have been writing a mystery novel. The original name I chose for my hero and detective was Felix Mock. Tell me if you remember where I might have gotten that name. (Don't you love that name? Kathy didn't like the name as much as I did so I changed it to something else.

Kathy is purchasing tickets for us to go to Opening Day here in Phoenix. She and her friend Deb (both former Cub fans together when they lived in Chicago) are going to a Spring Training game next week. Kathy loves this game of ball. One of the highlights of her whole last year was when you took her (and me) to a game at the old Yankee Stadium. She loves the subway, too.

I just got Skype, and I'm going to try to call you on it this week down in Mexico so I can get the hang of it. I know everyone else in the world knows how to use it. Looking forward to hearing your voice and hearing how you did filling in for Erica Jong at that writer's event.
   Love to Miranda,
   S.

[Editor's note: there is a famous baseball trivia question – Who is the only player ever to pinch hit for Ted Williams? The answer is Carroll Hardy, for whom trivia questions may have been invented. (He was also the only player to ever pinch hit for Carl Yastrzemski; and he also caught four touchdown passes for the San Francisco 49ers in 1955 thrown by Pro Football Hall-of-Famer Y.A. Tittle.) His gravestone will no doubt have the words "Once pinch hit for Ted Williams" on it.

My headstone will undoubtedly say, "Once pinch hit as a keynote speaker for Erica Jong." True. It was at the San Miguel Writers' Conference of 2009. Erica got sick at the last moment and couldn't come to San Miguel and I was asked to stand in, or speak in, or whatever the proper term would be. Anyway, that's what Steve's last paragraph in the above letter is a reference to. tnh.]

5 March – San Miguel de Allende, MX

steve,

Yes, of course I remember the name Felix Mock, though I don't think it's passed my lips for 45 years or so. He was a catcher on one of my baseball teams. Wasn't it the Wings in Babe Ruth League in Birmingham?

But that, you see, is what puzzles me. Because you weren't on the Wings were you? So how did you know Felix? Or was he on a different team with me, the one we played on together in Little League? I can't remember the name of the catcher on that team.

Still I do believe Felix Mock is a fitting name for a catcher. Or a sarcastic character in a Dickens novel. But not, I think, for a detective. Kathy's right on that; detectives do not "mock." Detectives are straight shooters, they talk blunt truth, they call a spade a spade.

Why don't you call your detective Sam Spade?

Discussing the name Mock reminds me how quickly we accept a name as a name, forgetting whatever other meaning the word might have. I'll give you several examples leading up to a funny one that happened just last week and tangentially involves you.

Okay:

When I was working at J. Walter Thompson we used to use a limo service called Vital Car Service to get to meetings. We were located at 43rd and Lexington in Midtown and it's very difficult to find a parking space around there so waiting limos would simply park (or double park) on nearby streets. So one afternoon in the pouring rain three of us dashed out the door of our office building, looking frantically (we were probably late) for the car we'd ordered. There was a long row of waiting limos, all of which looked the same. We couldn't find ours. One of the account women went from limo to limo in the driving rain shouting to the drivers through their closed windows and above the roar of the city: "Are you Vital?"

Let me just ask you, if you were a non-Vital limo driver, how would you answer that question?

Another example: as you know, we've lately been spending every fall at a cottage on Georgian Bay. It's in Tiny Township. For the most part, the people who live in the area no longer think of "tiny" as an adjective; for them, it's a place name. It is, therefore, only outsiders like us who find the name of a local storage business – Tiny Storage – amusing.

So here's the instance that happened the other day:

I met a woman at a party down here and was chatting with her over glasses of white wine and finger-sized empanadas. We were working our way through the usual San Miguel verbal feeling-out – where are you from originally? when did you come here? how do you know the host? do you think she's had plastic surgery? etc. – when all of a sudden the woman stopped, and with a look of recognition, says, "Oh, you're Two Guys!"

This outburst was, I believe, a reference to the fact that I am the co-author of the three "Two Guys" books rather than a suggestion that I'd put on too much weight. Still, it was kind of flattering that you and I had reached the stage where we are known by our brand, at least in the tonier barrios of San Miguel. I mean she was saying it in the same way she might have said, "Oh, you're Microsoft!" if she had suddenly realized she was talking to Bill Gates at a party.

Well … it's sort of the same.

terry.

15 March 2009 – San Miguel de Allende, MX

Steve,

We've been on a trip to Chiapas. My brother Chato read in a guidebook that Chiapas was dangerous and called us on our return for confirmation that we were still alive.

Yes, we are alive: we are, however, hostages.

Fortunately both my brothers will be down here next week; I hope they're bringing ransom money.

Back in December I read a *New York Times* story about a 73-year-old guy who went back to college and decided to go out for the basketball team. He made the team and actually played in a number of games during the season. Okay, so the name of the college was Roane State and not Duke or UCLA, still …

You can imagine the light bulb that went off in my head: I'm not 73; I'm only *64*! And basketball's not my best sport, but *baseball* is!

When you were down here in San Miguel I'm sure I showed you my gym which has, in addition to weights and some cardio equipment, a large outdoor paddleball court, virtually unused. Except by me.

Three years ago I devised a baseball throwing/fielding routine which I do there with my glove and a tennis ball. It's basically 200 throws a day, but it includes 30 from deep to my right, another 30 from deep to my left plus 30 hard from close range to work on my reflexes. The last two years it was only 150 throws but this year I stepped it up to 200 after reading the *Times* story. My footwork's now on a par with Luis Aparicio's during his Gold Glove years.

I was thinking that Derek Jeter's a lot more fragile than he used to be – he could go down at any time during the season. The Yankees have my phone number down here. I know this because I've left it with the operator at their office several times as well as giving her a brief description of my workout.

Look, I know you're saying that 162 games is a long, hard haul and I agree. At 64, maybe my body can't take that kind of pounding, but for 30 or 40 games … hey, c'mon. And, yes, I also know it'd take some extra BP the first couple of days to sharpen my hitting eye; I'm not going into this with unrealistic expectations.

Anyway, while I was down in Chiapas, I picked up a copy of Mexico's English-language newspaper (called *El News*) and my Yankee heart sank to read that A-Rod's got a bum hip and will miss a month or six weeks of the season after arthroscopic surgery. Damn! Just when we had all the pieces in place to walk away with the pennant.

I immediately went to the Yankee team page on mlb.com and checked the depth chart at third base. So the guy who's gonna take A-Rod's place is a 33-year-old utility player named Cody Ransom. It doesn't even sound like a ball player's name, more like the name of a side character in a "Spin and Marty" episode. In parts of six seasons in the Bigs, this guy's played a grand total of 7 major league games at third base. 7!!!

What really bothered me is that I'm a natural shortstop and not a third baseman. But then it hit me: The Yankees could solve their problem *by moving Jeter over to third.* Then short would be open *and* the Yankees have my phone number!

Anyway, while I was in Chiapas, my daily exercise was a fast 3-mile walk instead of my baseball workout because I didn't have access to a gym with a paddleball court – plus I hadn't packed my glove. So I came back to San Miguel anxious to get back into my baseball workout. Now here's the part you have to keep quiet: three days ago while doing my workout, I sprained my ankle and it's still kinda ouchy. Don't get me wrong, I can still play. But keep it under your hat because obviously the Yankees won't call me up if they think I'm damaged goods.

Okay, so that gets to your question of the previous e-mail: can throwing money at a problem make it go away? I'm surprised you don't know the answer to this, Steve. Yes, definitely. And frankly, I won't cost that much.

I am not as definite on your other question as to whether steroids helped A-Rod. Although I have done extensive analysis.

On the surface, yes. Taking the three years before he used steroids and the three years after, he averaged about 40.6 homers per season. The three years *with* the enhanced swing – he averaged 52.

But unfortunately the three years he was using steroids coincide with the only three years he was with the Texas Rangers and I don't know enough about their park to know *its* effect on his numbers.

The one *I* want to know about – and no one, to my knowledge, has ever questioned this – is Brady Anderson. Remember him? He was famous for his sideburns, but he was a very good outfielder in the majors for 15 seasons. I believe he is the only man – outside of the steroids-pumped Barry Bonds (seriously, can any reasonable man doubt it?) – ever to steal 50 bases in a season *and* hit 50 home runs in a season. Neither Barry nor Brady did it in the *same* season, but they both did it.

Let's take a look at that though. 1996 was the year Brady hit 50 homers. The year before he hit 16; the year after, he hit 18. His best year *ever*, outside of '96, he hit 24! As the Youngbloods once sang: "Something's happenin' here / What it is ain't exactly clear."

Well, it might not have been exactly clear *then*; we were all innocents then. But it seems pretty clear to me *now*. The main item for the defense would have to be a *Baseball Encyclopedia* with the page open to Norm Cash's stats.

"Would your Honor please take a look at Mr. Cash's 1961 season?"

That year Cash hit .361 – 75 points higher than he ever did before or after. Go figure.

Sincerely, Walter Mitty.

16 March 2009 - Tucson, Arizona

Terry,

We spent the weekend here in Tucson at the Festival of Books where poet laureate Billy Collins and I were featured authors giving talks. The festival (which is to say Billy and I, really) drew 50,000 book fans over two days! Who says books are no longer popular?

Okay, I'll have to confess that there were 340 other authors at this massive event. I myself was sponsored by the BBC which has produced three of my audiobooks, and when Kathy and I met our BBC contact Michelle, the first thing I asked her was whether she could get me an introduction to Helen Mirren. An embarrassing request, looking back.

There was a synchronicity in Tucson! The morning of our departure from the hotel I was reading your father's book on baseball, *I Don't Care If I Ever Come Back*, and had just finished the chapter about his father (your grandfather, whom I remember well from our boyhood days) being captain of the University of Michigan baseball team. I then packed your dad's book into my suitcase and got on the elevator to leave and who should join me on the elevator but three big young athletes with University of Michigan athletic gear on! They were on the U of Michigan baseball team! In Arizona! I asked one of the guys, who looked to be a coach, how playing baseball in Ann Arbor was in March and he said they practiced, of course, indoors. But they were here to play the Arizona Wildcats out of doors in lovely 75-degree sunshine. As we got into our car we saw them get on the bus to ride over to the ballpark to play. Goosebump coincidence!

S.

17 March 2009 – Gilbert, Arizona

Hi Terry....

Back home in Gilbert I see that Arizona beat Michigan in baseball that day 14–0. But poor Michigan was unaccustomed to playing out of doors and it was probably very disorienting to do so. ("I lost the ball in the sun!")

I loved picturing you in Mexico throwing a tennis ball against the wall and catching it at age 64! 200 times a day! When you and I were both 11 years old we used to cut open golf balls, remember? We'd take a knife and cut through the plastic outer coating and then watch the little compacted rubber bands snap and pop off revealing the core little rubber ball in the center. We'd then use that hard little ball to throw at walls and catch in our gloves. And because that ball had such amazing bounce, we'd learn very rapid responses with our gloves.

And now 53 years later a lonely man in Mexico on an abandoned paddle ball court fires and retrieves, fires and retrieves, brooding about Rodriguez. I can't wait for the actual season to start!

Give my love to Miranda, and thank her for showing us how to link up for our Skype call last week. It was good talking to you and knowing you had arrived home safely from Chiapas. Have they declared martial law in Mexico yet? I heard a rumor. Really I'm not kidding. I know how you love to joke about death, violence and tragedy, but try to be safe.

Take care, s.

31 March 2009 – New York, NY

Dear Steve,

After three months in Mexico, we're back home in the land of the Yankees and the Mets. We got to our apartment in the early evening and by 9:30 I'd seen my first major league baseball of the year on television.

After unpacking a bit, we took a walk in the neighborhood to see what'd changed. As we walked I could see a lot of televisions through the windows of bars and cafes and noticed there was a Mets game on.

Back at the apartment, we ordered Chinese food and turned on the game. The score was 1–1 in the 7th. This should be exciting, right?

No.

Because it is a spring training game. Spring training games are never interesting to me because they don't count. The managers aren't really trying to win. They just want a good look at their players with an eye to what they might be able to do when the season starts. The players aren't really trying to win either. They're trying to make the team, or to get in shape for the games that *do* count.

I feel much the same about the All-Star Game. I don't believe I've watched more than five innings *total* of the last 20 All-Star Games. If you want proof that even Major League Baseball doesn't care who wins the All-Star Game, I offer the evidence of the game several years ago that was running late when it went into extra innings, so the *Commissioner* of Baseball simply declared it a tie. A tie? Well, if *he* doesn't care if there's a winner or not, why should I?

Having said all that about how little interest I have in exhibition games, I must say I loved watching the last three innings of the game last night. There were a couple of interesting defensive plays and the Mets pulled it out with a run in the 8th. Plus it was just nice seeing a ballgame again. But while watching the game I was reminded what an imperfect match baseball is with television. Don't get me wrong, if they're gonna televise the games, I'm gonna watch – and be grateful. But I'd rather be there in person.

A baseball game on television is like watching the Battle of Gettysburg shot with two cameras. You might get some good action, but you miss a lot. Just one small example from last night: In the bottom of the 7th, with the score tied, Carlos Beltran led off the inning with a single. Beltran, who at this point represents the winning run for the Mets, is speedy; the man stole 25 bases last year. Wouldn't you think he might be going? If I were at the game I would have been keeping half an eye on him while watching the batter and pitcher. Eventually, when the count was 3–2, he *did* go. But I had to be told about it by the announcer instead of seeing it, because the camera was following the pitch.

It's true you miss the replays when you're at the game. And I admit, I love the replays. (The Union soldiers must have watched that Pickett's charge replay a hundred times on You Tube.) In fact, the winning run last night was scored on a play that I only really understood after I saw the replay. Fernando Tatis (last year's "Comeback Player of the Year") hit a drive deep to right-center and he went for a triple. When the throw came in for the play at third, it was either a bit off line, or the third baseman just missed it. At any rate it skittered into the dugout and the umpire waved Tatis home with the winning run.

It was only when you saw the replay that you realized that the throw had actually grazed Tatis arm and this had caused the ball to change course and skip past the fielder. If you'd been at the game you never would have known that until you read the interview with Tatis in the paper the next day. Still I would rather have been eating peanuts and Cracker Jacks.

Opening Day's only six days away!

terry.

April 1, 2009 – Gilbert, Arizona

Dear Terry,

Glad that you are back in the USA, home in Greenwich Village, (where Joan Baez and Bob Dylan got their starts as folksingers around Washington Square) and ready for the season to start.

Dylan has a new album coming out in a couple weeks, and that's always a cause for celebration to me, given that he's now the most humorously poetic grumpy old man who ever lived. The new album has a title that you and I (having been friends for 54 years) can relate to: *Together Through Life*.

Bob Dylan loves baseball and did a whole show on the subject on his Theme Time Radio Hour show. It featured Bob himself singing "Take Me Out to the Ballgame," and a host of other songs about baseball, including Sonny Rollins' classic, "Newk's Fadeaway."

(About Don Newcombe's pitch.)

You've been in Mexico, so you might not have received the news about the death of Whitey Lockman last week. He was 82, so that's a pretty good life (although I'm aiming to live longer than that given some projects I'm working on that will require it). You and I had Whitey's baseball card when we were young and he was a Giant first baseman. I can still picture his card.

He's best remembered for his role in the shot heard around the world. In the playoff game that would decide who was going to the World Series in1951, Whitey's Giants were behind 4–1 in the bottom of the ninth. Don Newcombe was on the mound for the Dodgers. Runners on first and third with one out. Whitey sees that Newcombe's second pitch is coming in high and outside ... it's Newk's fadeaway! Whitey Lockman, God rest his soul, smacked the pitch into left field just inside the foul line, and by the time Andy Pafko had chased it down, Whitey had a double, making the score 4–2. You know the rest. They took Newk out, put in Ralph Branca, and Bobby Thompson hit the home run heard around the world and sent the Giants into the World Series.

But here's the interesting part. As exciting as that home run was, (and we've all heard that famous recording of the announcer going wild), Lockman didn't have a totally happy memory of it. Why? He injured his shoulder and neck badly while helping his teammates lift Thompson over their heads.

This little anecdote confirms the worried feeling I always get when I watch ballplayers piling on top of each other to celebrate a win. Who will get hurt in this pile up? I think more get hurt than we hear about. Because no one wants to go public with the news that they were injured celebrating.

A few years back, our own Arizona Cardinals football team's field goal kicker Martin Grammatica injured himself celebrating a field goal he kicked in the first quarter against the New York (football) Giants. The little guy threw up his arms joyfully and hopped around like Russ Tamblyn playing Tom Thumb and tore his ACL. His career was never the same after that. He ended up in the now-defunct Arena Football League.

It's amazing that a field goal kicker can get injured but even more so when you see a manager, like Roger Craig, show up in uniform for a game with a heavily bandaged hand as he did in 1992. The cause? He had cut his hand ... very badly it turns out ... the night before on a bra strap. No further details available. Baseball may be the ultimate aphrodisiac.

Monday I'll be in the stands in Phoenix watching the Arizona Diamondbacks on Opening Day. You never know what could happen. But I'll write you.

s.

6 April 2009 (Opening Day) – NYC, NY

Steve,

Yes, I am aware that the Braves opened the season yesterday by beating the Phillies in Philadelphia. But as far as I'm concerned, opening day is the day your own team plays their first game – and that's today. The Yankees play the Orioles in Baltimore. And the Mets are in Cincinnati to face the Reds. I'll be watching both on television while you're in your air-conditioned Phoenix stadium watching the Diamondbacks.

I'm glad the Mets and Yankees are both playing away today because they'd be rained out if they were at home. It's cold and rainy here, but the temperature's fine in our apartment.

The only real opening game I ever saw in person was the 1977 Toronto Blue Jays opener.

Memorable because a rookie first baseman named Doug Ault hit two homers for the Blue Jays that day to give Toronto the win. (That was the game Ault will remember on his deathbed. In his entire three-plus-year career he only hit 17 homers.)

Memorable because the temperature was in the mid-30s and the field was covered with snow.

Memorable because it was the very first game the Blue Jays ever played.

Many years later I saw a "home" opener in Detroit that my brother Chato got me tickets to. After seeing dozens of games at Briggs/Tiger Stadium, this was the first time I ever saw a game in the Tigers' new home – Comerica Park. And as much as I love the old Tiger Stadium for all its associations, I have to say that the new stadium is a terrific place to watch a game. Comerica is built on the "retro" model that became popular after Baltimore's Camden Yards opened in the early '90s. It's also what the new Mets Stadium is based on.

So I guess actually I've only seen a couple of opening games in the last 50 years. Compare that with Chato, who's seen about 35.

It started in junior high school when he was maybe 13. His birthday is March 29th and he'd received some birthday money as a present that year. On opening day in the middle of the morning he just walked out of school (Derby Junior High), caught a bus to downtown Detroit and went to the game. As I recall, back then the bus downtown was 55 cents and you could get into the bleachers for another 50 cents. (Shoot me if I say, "Those were the days.")

It started a tradition. All the rest of the way through junior high and high school he'd skip school on opening day and go see the Tigers. His written excuse to get into school the next day was always "written" by my father, whose handwriting and signature Chato's still strongly resembles to this day.

Even after he started working, Chato kept up the opening game tradition as often as he could. Once when he was working at a Detroit advertising agency, his picture was featured in a photo essay in the morning *Detroit Free Press* about opening day. When he arrived at work that day, the picture was cut out and mounted on his office wall with the caption: "I will not be in this afternoon as I will be attending my grandmother's funeral."

Starting at 4pm this afternoon, I will also be at the funeral. Don't call. Terry.

Text Message to Steve – April 6th, 8:05 pm.

DID YOU HEAR THE YANKEES WON'T BE SERVING BEER AT THE STADIUM THIS YEAR? TERRY.

Text Message to Terry – April 6th, 8:13 pm.

WHY?   STEVE.

Text Message to Steve – April 6th, 8:16 pm.

THEY LOST THE OPENER.   TERRY.

7 April 2009 – New York, NY

Steve,

I must admit that is one of my favorite jokes, but of course, it can't be used unless your team loses the opener. Making it a bit of a mixed blessing.

Living in New York naturally gives you two teams that could lose the opener. This greatly increases your chances of being able to tell that joke each year. Which is, of course, the main reason I moved to New York from Toronto.

That and women problems.

But nobody wants to hear women problems. They'd rather hear the joke.

Yes, the Yankees lost the opener. Giving up 10 runs in the process. The good news is that only 9 of them were earned runs; however, unfortunately this still leaves them with a team ERA of 10.13. And that's *not* good news, because I can't remember the last team to win the pennant with an ERA over 10.

I have an addiction that the baseball season feeds. It's an addiction to stories.

I know that in one of your books you wrote quite a bit about the importance and power of stories. I believe that. But my addiction has nothing to do with any of that. I just want to know what happens next and how it ends. Miranda jokes that flipping through television channels she cannot pause for even a couple of seconds on any channel because I'll inevitably get hooked. It doesn't matter how dumb the show is, if I catch a whiff of a storyline, I want to follow my nose and find out what happens next.

The baseball season is a story. It takes seven months to tell and there's a beginning and a middle and an end. That's pretty straightforward and I love it. But, of course, each game is a story too. A multi-textured story with a hundred sub-plots.

If you say to me "bottom of the eighth, score tied 1–1, runner on third, one out" … well that's like a red cape to me. I need to know what happens next. I can't tell you how many times I've tuned in a game on TV just to get the score and then wound up watching the last hour of the game.

But anyway, the season is started and I'm happy.

Once upon a time …

t.

April 7, 2009 – Phoenix, Arizona

Dear Terry,

Kathy and I and our friend Deb Bailly were among the 48,000 plus
people to fill up Chase Field in Phoenix for Opening Day. A sunshiny
(what day isn't in Arizona?) Monday afternoon. Our Diamondbacks
were playing the Colorado Rockies.

This is only the 11th season for the Diamondbacks, and the team
has already won five Cy Young awards, so the pitching here is usually
good. Hitting has been the problem in recent years, and that's not
much fun for a fan. To watch your team not score runs. I mean, how
could it possibly be fun? You pay your money to watch someone do
something. You sit down. And they don't do it. For three hours they
don't do it, and you're watching all the while. Then you go home.

You see your doctor the next morning. He notices that you are a
little depressed. He pulls his prescription pad out and writes you a
prescription. He warns you that the drug may trigger suicidal ideation.
Or even sudden death. You ask why that would be better than just being
mildly depressed and he says, "Just give it a try." Your downward
spiral begins. And it's all because your favorite players refuse to take
extra batting practice in the off-season.

But this game was not like that! The first Arizona batter of the
season, Felipe Lopez, stepped up to the plate and hit a home run. Our
great pitcher Brandon Webb got hammered by the Rockies, but it
didn't matter because our hitters were on fire. Old Tony Clark hit two
home runs and so did young Lopez. Tony Clark only hit three homers
last year and Lopez only hit six.

Lopez's favorite song – "This Is Why I'm Hot" – a rap song,
played over the loud speakers each time he stepped up to the plate. It
was an appropriate song for him on opening day.

The Diamondbacks won 9–8!

One thing our home team Diamondbacks finally noticed after

choosing its unique nickname eleven years ago is that the name has a lot of letters in it. Eleven letters is a lot to fit across the front of a uniform! So they began calling them the "D-Backs." Or, sometimes, just The Snakes.

It was good that the game was wild with lots of scoring and cheering because I originally went into the stadium very tired ... we had been up quite late the night before watching Leonard Cohen perform at the Dodge Theater, and he kept coming back for encore after encore. An amazing performance for a 75-year-old man. He said the last time he did a live tour like this was way back when he was 60 ... "Back when I was just a crazy kid with a big dream," he said. He acknowledged that the whole world was in a recession now. "Times are rather tricky right now," he said. "But we've been through difficult times before. Remember Y2K? Now that was rough."

The crowd went nuts for Leonard all night long, and he was back for so many encores that we finally had to leave. Too much of a good thing. And we knew we had opening day the next day and that we needed to be sharp for that.

When you mentioned the snow-covered Toronto opening day with the improbable Doug Ault hitting two homers, I saw the coincidental parallel there with the improbable Felipe Lopez. Which is why baseball is such an interesting game. You never know. Nothing like the college basketball championship game played on TV the same night ... because you already knew that North Carolina was going to crush Michigan State. Which they did. Unlike other sports, baseball is wonderfully unpredictable.

I remember going with you to Blue Jay games in Toronto when you lived there. Back in the 1970s. And I also remember going to watch you play in softball games in the Toronto Press League. Many years have passed, and still there's baseball.

Two tunes stayed in my mind as we left the happy, victorious ballpark. 1) "Take Me Out to the Ballgame," which we sang in 48,000-part harmony in the 7th inning. And 2) "This Is Why I'm Hot," the Lopez song. ("This is why I'm hot/ this is why I'm hot/ I'm hot because I'm fly / you ain't because you're not.") Hard to get that out of your head.

love to you and Miranda,
Steve

PS- I sent you some dice today that I bought for you in Las Vegas a couple weeks ago. Long story. Let me know if you get them. They have your name on them, which I hope you notice.

10 April 2009 – New York, NY

Steve,

Chase Field in Phoenix. I assume its name is a tribute to the great first baseman Hal Chase. Chase was in the majors from 1905–1919 and many consider him the greatest fielding first baseman not only of *his* time but of *all*-time. But he also hit well enough to have won the National League batting championship in 1916. The team he is most associated with is the New York Highlanders, which later became the Yankees.

He is not in the Hall of Fame probably because he sometimes took money to throw games. He was basically blackballed from major league baseball in 1920, but stayed in baseball when he managed a professional team in Douglas, Arizona. I think it's great that the city of Phoenix has honored his memory by naming its stadium after him.

(You know after I wrote that it occurred to me that maybe Chase Field was *not* named after Hal Chase. Maybe it was named after the Chase Bank. But then I thought, what a stupid notion. I mean what does a bank have to do with baseball? Why would they name a baseball park after a bank? Anyway, since I'm planning on visiting you next month, I'm looking forward to visiting Hal Chase Field and seeing a game with you there. I assume there'll be a statue of Hal at the entrance to the stadium.)

Earlier today, by the way, the Detroit Tigers won their home opener 15–2. As you may have guessed Chato was there. I believe our grandmother died; she's getting used to it.

I am ashamed to admit, Steve, that for the Diamondbacks' entire existence as a baseball team I have been misspelling their name. The worst part is that I'm not sure how. You see when I spell it, it has 12 letters, not 11. What's the extra letter I'm putting in there?

The dice arrived in the mail today, and yes, they do have my name on them. Thanks.

I assume you sent them to me so that I could start another dice-game baseball league like we had when we were kids. In fact I'd love to, but I simply don't have the time anymore.

Do you remember my four-team league that I had for several years when we were in junior high? The four teams were called the Cats, the Dogs, the Jets, and the Bruts. The league was a few games into my first season when you cruelly pointed out to me that Brutes was spelled with an "e." It was really too late for me to change the name; the team had already played four or five games so I merely changed the way I was pronouncing it, moving from a long "u" to a short "u" and that became the name of the team for the duration of the league … several years.

It wasn't until I noticed your miscounting of the letters in Diamondbacks in your last e-mail that I was able to render payback for your willful cruelty when we were 12 years old.

t.

11 April 2009 – AZ

Dear Terry,

Glad you got the dice … I bought them for you in a gift shop in Vegas where Kathy and I went to hear Neil Sedaka. (He was amazing … in his 70s but with a pure, true tenor voice that just rocked and soared all night.) I hoped you would relate the dice to the baseball card games you and I played as kids. And you did.

Thanks for telling me about Hal Chase. If all he did was take money to throw games, then his would be a more honorable name to have on our park – much more honor there than naming it after a recession-producing bank of today. So I will begin a local movement to retain the name Chase Field but have the name hereafter refer to Hal. Nobody's perfect.

Go Dimondbacks! s.

12 April 2009 – Gilbert, Arizona

Dear Terry,

Thanks for the phone call. It was fun planning your visit here in May. Sorry to hear you left your baseball glove in Mexico; how do you exercise in New York without it? But, yes, I'll have a couple of gloves for us so we can toss to each other.

My mother-in-law Jeanne and I were talking yesterday about your visit and this book, and she expressed an interest in going to the batting cages with us and taking some swings. She was worried though that the balls would be coming in 90 miles an hour at major league speed and that might be intimidating for her. Given that she is 84 years old I agreed that she might not get the bat around on a 90-mile-an-hour pitch as she would have in the past. But she was delighted to hear that these cages also have slow pitch softball cages that anyone can hit in. Kathy and I have had fun there.

Thanks for talking about your addiction to stories. I would call this a positive addiction. (William Glasser wrote a good book called *Positive Addiction* in which he talks about life-enhancing addictions like running, reading and playing music.) Just today I received in the mail a book called *STORY* by screenwriter Robert McKee. I'd owned this book before, years ago, when our friend Fred Knipe gave it to me. Fred was writing a play at the time and swore by it. And because I am now writing a mystery novel (uncharted waters for me), I need to read it again.

Speaking of Fred, he and I are writing songs together again. After all these years. One of the fun parts of a recession is that it gets you to thinking more innovatively than in lazier times. Like, "How else can I make a little money? What are some alternative ways to create some wealth?"

Fred and I have made royalties in the past by writing songs, so why not pull out the old guitar, dust it off, put on some new strings and write something? Who is stopping me?

So today I worked on the song, "That's How the Future Used to Be." Fred makes his living as a comedian, but he has dusted off his guitar now too. Our music will rise up from this recession! Fred's been taking extra trips to Nashville and meeting with other songwriters, producers and music publishers. He recently got our song, "I Can't Get to You From Here" placed with George Strait.

There will be two guitars here newly strung and tuned for your arrival in May. Two gloves, too.

Steve

ps- I'm sorry you rejected my proposed title for this book *Two Guys Steal Home*. Especially my concept for it that "stealing home" be a metaphor for dying. In the tradition of the promotion-oriented baseball team owner Bill Veeck, I thought we might stage our own deaths in the book, and have our wives finish writing it.

But the plan wasn't a good one. I'll admit it. They wouldn't go along, our wives. I don't think they thought it was that funny when during the photo shoot for *Two Guys Read the Obituaries* you and I lay down on the grass in Mexico and closed our eyes and opened our mouths pretending to have passed away. (When I reminded Kathy of this incident she said, "Maybe our displeasure was that you guys *got up*.")

15 April 2009 – NYC, NY

Steve,

The new star of the Yankees is the unlikely Nick Swisher. During the off-season he was signed as a free agent to help make up for the offense we'd lose with the departures of Jason Giambi and Bobby Abreu. At the time they were concentrating on getting free-agent pitchers. But then they surprised everyone including themselves by the signing of Mark Teixeira; suddenly Swisher wasn't really needed. I'll bet they wished they could get out of the deal. For the first two games of the season Swisher was on the bench.

But eight games into the season, the guy leads the team in batting average, home runs, runs batted in … *and earned run average*!

This last unlikely stat came about a couple of days ago when the Yankees were down by 10 runs to the Rays in the eighth. Manager Joe Girardi didn't want to waste a real pitcher for the mop-up job so he called on Swisher to pitch. Swisher got through the inning without giving up a run. So his ERA is 0.00, tying him with Mariano Rivera for best on the team.

While he was pitching Swisher did things like shaking off a lot of the catcher's signs when Molina wasn't actually giving him any. Also at one point he actually struck out a player and when he got the ball back he rolled it over to the dugout to have them save it for his trophy case.

So Swisher's a hot dog. But right now they aren't calling him that because you don't call a guy hitting .468 a hot dog. They're saying he's "colorful" instead. After all, he's about the only thing the Yankees have had to cheer about so far.

Chien-Ming Wang, Miranda's favorite pitcher for obvious reasons, has started two games for us and so far has an ERA of 28.93. To break this down for our readers, this means that in a nine-inning game he'd give up 29 runs.

It puts an awful strain on your hitters to have to score 30 runs to win the game each time Chien-Ming pitches.

My earlier-stated fears about Cody Ransom being our regular third baseman in A-Rod's absence have proven well-founded. The man is currently hitting .083. This really hurts a team that's trying to hang 30 runs on the scoreboard. Maybe they should sit him out the days Chien-Ming starts.

Or maybe …

They should move Jeter over to third and call *me* up for short. Rodriguez is due back in 30 days and I know my body would hold up for that long. Yes, you're right that since I've been back in New York I haven't been doing my baseball workout, but I have been doing my daily 3-mile walk and I just joined a gym here. So I'm ready.

t.

16 April 2009 – Gilbert Arizona

Terry,

Thank you for telling me about the dashing and daring Swisher! He *is* a colorful character, and I love that in sports. You and I are hot dogs, too, are we not? In our respective professions? Be honest. In our personal lives, too? Tell the truth.

Strange happening: I had become so frustrated following the hitless wonders sometimes known as the D-Backs, that I thought I'd take a break from baseball and settle into the latest Robert Parker crime novel with Jesse Stone as the main character. But in the chapter I'm on now I read that Stone had a photo of Ozzie Smith on his wall in his home. (Smith was the great Cardinal shortstop known as The Wizard of Oz.) And in the scene Jesse Stone is troubled by a complicated crime and starts talking to the picture on the wall! Just like I talk to the TV screen! And he says, "Used to be simpler, Oz. Used to be about whether you could go to the right and make the long throw. Used to be about whether you could sit on the fastball and adjust for the curve."

Later on Robert Parker muses, "Baseball was the most important thing that didn't matter that he'd ever known."

Steve

17 April 2009 – Gilbert, Arizona

Ter,

I wake up. I make coffee. I walk the long walk down the driveway to get the paper. Birds singing. Sweet breezes blowing. It's April in Arizona. What could go wrong? Nothing ... until I actually read the paper. There's an interview in it with one of the struggling young hitters on our struggling baseball team.

This hitter hit .109 in Cactus League play this spring, and has dipped to .105 in the regular season (in the regular season pitchers are now bearing down more seriously, which explains his troubling loss of batting average points.)

But here's what I hate. Even more than his lack of hitting. (They have said he's the next Willie Mays.) I hate the second person. In interviews. I have always hated the second person. Not just in interviews, but in any conversation. And by second person I mean the repeated use of the word "you" instead of "I." It is a total no-responsibility wimp-out.

So they ask this young potential star about his hitting and the possibility of sending him to AAA minors for a tune-up. He rolls his eyes. (Like, that would be so stupid! Send me down? It's not like I'm hitting .005. I've had hits. Two, in fact.) Then he uses the second person. Which you now know I hate. He says, "Sometimes you fall into bad habits."

He's talking about "the mechanics of his swing" it turns out. But he says sometimes YOU fall into bad habits. Why couldn't he say sometimes "I" fall into bad habits? Because he wants to include the interviewer. And he wants to include everyone else listening to the interview. It's not just him. Look at everybody's swing!

The University of Arizona had a football coach once who used the second person more than anyone in the history of Western Civilization. Everything he said was second person. It was as if he had no life of his own. Therefore no responsibility.

"You never want to lose a game like that." "You try to call the plays your team knows how to run." "You always want to recruit well in your home town." A reporter would ask him, "Are, you, Coach, personally happy, with the contract the University has offered you?" And he would say, "You feel a certain pride even being in the PAC-10 conference. You always hope for more money, but you are satisfied, in the end, to be coaching the sport you love."

The reporter asks him, "Why did you take the quarterback out in the third quarter?" "You want to give your backups a chance," he would say. He was a master deflector to the second person.

If I were the reporter, I would say to the young Diamondback hitter, after he said "Sometimes you fall into bad habits," "Do I? How did you know that about me? But you're right! Sometimes I leave my notebook in the car and have to borrow one for an interview! What else do you know about me?" And if the football coach said, "You want to give your backups a chance," I would say, "My backups? Why would I want to give them a chance, coach? I just want it to be me here, asking YOU why YOU took your quarterback out."

Why have I not used the actual names of these people I am quoting? Well! You don't want to offend people unnecessarily.

S.

19 April 2009 – Toronto, Canada

steve,

Miranda and I flew into Toronto yesterday and checked into our hotel at just about 12:30. We dropped our bags in our room and walked to the Blue Jays stadium, bought nosebleed seats from a scalper for eight bucks apiece and went to my first big league game of the year: Blue Jays versus the Oakland Athletics.

The first pitch was scheduled for 1:07 so we even had a chance to enjoy a street hot dog before going into the stadium. The street dogs in Toronto are *without a doubt* the best of any city I've ever been to. They are spectacular. They are also about half the price of the dogs you can buy in the stadium and approximately twice as good.

The Toronto stadium, which was hailed as the eighth wonder of the modern world when it was built in 1989 and was then called the SkyDome, is the worst stadium in baseball now. It's made entirely of plastic (including the "grass") and painted in a synthetic-looking blue giving it the feel of a very large Fisher-Price toy. For three consecutive years in the early '90s the Blue Jays drew more than 4 million fans a season. In none of the last ten years have they been able to draw even 2 million. The good side of that is that I'm able to pick up $8 tickets.

Looking around this plastic palace, I felt there *might* have been 15,000 people in the place. In fact, the official number I saw this morning in the paper was 21,698. Everybody does this now; have you noticed? They inflate the attendance numbers and then have all kinds of fudgy explanations when pressed by reporters who believe their eyes rather than the team's "official" numbers.

Still, as bad as the stadium is, as bad as their fan support is, they still play nine innings and the team with the most runs at the end of the game still wins so I'm there. And it was a great game! Extra innings with the Blue Jays (who are in first place in the American League East as I write) winning 4–2 on a homer by Lyle Overbay with two out in the bottom of the 12th.

Jason Giambi, who was greeted by taunting chants of "ster-oids, ster-oids" every time he came to bat, drove in both of the A's runs. I note, however, that the man with 396 lifetime homers hasn't hit a single one yet this season.

Every time he came to bat, the Jays put on the Giambi Shift, with three infielders playing between first and second. Okay, that's Jason Giambi; but they also used the shift on some guy named Jack Cust. Jack Cust? The Cust Shift? And tell me one thing, Steve, why can't professional hitters manage to hit the ball to the left side of the infield when the shift is on?

While we watched the game, we kept one eye on the scoreboard to see how the Mets and the Yankees were doing. The Mets with Santana pitching won 1–0. The Yankee game started later and we were encouraged when they got two runs in the first to take a 2–0 lead. But we had not factored in that Chien-Ming Wang was pitching for us. At the end of two, the score was Yankees 2, Indians 14! Yes, Cleveland got 14 runs in the second.

Wang's ERA is now at 34.50. It really is too much to expect your hitters to produce 35 runs every time Wang pitches.

There has been a lot of talk about how many home runs are being hit this year. But I haven't heard anyone comment on how many shutouts have been pitched. I've seen no statistics on it, but just looking at the box scores every day it just seems that there've been a lot more than the norm.

Yesterday, for instance, there were six. But, Steve, these aren't the shutouts we remember from our youth. Only one of yesterday's shutouts was a complete game by a starting pitcher. Four of them, in fact, involved three pitchers combining for the shutout.

t.

29 April 2009 – Gilbert, Arizona

Dear Terry,

Your depiction of Toronto's baseball stadium was funny. Like sitting in a big plastic toy. When you and I played as kids, baseball was always about grass, and dirt and wood and leather. A game made up of authentic outdoor elements.

Some of the newer stadiums are going back to that: brick and mortar and lime. Grass and open skies and the crack of a wooden bat. (I can't stand the metal bats used in college these days ... even the sound when the ball is struck is not baseball to me.)

But outside the park in Toronto? The best hot dogs in the world! (And I know you are a world connoisseur.) So Emerson's essay called "Compensation" is validated once again. For every "bad" thing in life, something good compensates for it. That was his main point. Or, as Julie Andrews said in *The Sound of Music*, "When the good Lord closes a door, He always opens a window." (You don't have to read Emerson if you watch the right movies.)

We bought the tickets to the Diamondbacks game you'll be watching with us here ... it's a beautiful park; you will love it. We will be playing the Washington Nationals. Why didn't they take their old name (the team in DC when you and I were young) – the Washington Senators? Well. Why give a team a negative name?

Looking forward to your visit. Please place Kentucky Derby bets for me and Kathy as you do every year at the Off Track window in NYC. I'm choosing Pioneer of the Nile and Kathy selects Musket Man.

love to Miranda, Steve.

4 May 2009 – New York City

steve,

The great thing about living in New York during baseball season (well, *one* of the great things) is that there are two games to watch on television virtually every day. Walking around the neighborhood in the evenings you can check the progress of the games simply by looking in the doors or windows of bars at the big flat screen TVs because they all have the games on. Even on traditional off-days, usually one or the other of the New York teams is playing.

Last night was an exception. Both the Yankees and the Mets were rained out. It felt strange.

This morning there were no Yankee or Mets box scores to review so I set about getting the big picture on the season so far by studying the standings. Can you believe they've already played basically one-sixth of the season?

None of our teams is happy right now: your D-Backs are 11–14 and you seem to have lost your ace pitcher. The Mets are marginally worse at 10–13, but it feels *a lot* worse because everyone had picked them to win the NL-East.

On the surface, you'd think the Yankees would be relatively happy at 13–10 without A-Rod, but it's a discouraging 13–10. When they were 9–6 and seemed ready to make a run for the league lead, they went to Boston for a three-game series. They got swept.

But it was because of the *way* they were swept that we wept.

The Yankees led in all three games. In the first game they led 4–2 with two outs in the 9th and the best reliever in baseball on the mound. A 2-run homer by Jason Bay tied it and the Sox won it in the 11th on another home run.

In the second, the Yanks led 6–0 in the 4th and then again 10–9 in the 7th. Neither lead held up and they lost 16–11. The third game didn't feature any big collapse – they just lost. It was humiliating.

But I'm ever optimistic. A-Rod's due back in days. They brought Phil Hughes up from the minors and he very successfully stepped in for what should have been Wang's last start. And at the end of the day, they're 13–10. Tonight begins a three game home series against ... the Boston Red Sox.

Payback time!

terry.

5 May 2009 – Gilbert AZ.

Dear Terry,

Long ago I worked as a sportswriter for the daily *Tucson Citizen*. Last week that paper died. It closed its doors forever. Rest in peace.

This morning my newspaper here in Phoenix showed signs of being terminally ill. I went down the driveway and picked it up in anticipation of reading about last night's game and the sports page said, "Last night's Dodgers-Diamondbacks game finished too late for our press run. To read about it ..." And then they gave the website of the paper. The website! I threw the paper across the room. I then went to ESPN.com. D-backs lost 7–2. I thought, this day can only get better.

If you can get your news instantly on the internet why would you be patient with a newspaper that can't get it to you at all? Newspapers are like 8-track tapes. Their time has come and gone. I want to be Zen and accept it as good. All form dissolves. When the good Lord closes a door, you can always open Windows.

    s.

7 May 2009 – Los Angeles, California

Steve,

Baseball is so much a part of the American scene that it has laced itself through our language. We so take this for granted that we don't even notice we're using baseball metaphors. But imagine, for instance, what Europeans or new students of English coming from countries where baseball is not the national pastime would make of such expressions as "Obama really hit a home run with his Inaugural Address."

Or "Rubin was way off base with his economic plan."

Or "Well that idea came out of left field."

Or "He's been out with her three times and he hasn't even gotten to second base."

Or "Bill was sick so John had to pinch-hit for him at the meeting."

Or "I thought everything was settled, but we got thrown a curve."

And a thousand others. To explain them all to a foreigner, you'd have to explain baseball, which isn't easy to do. (Do you remember that Bob Newhart skit about an executive at a game company who's pitched the idea of baseball? He thinks he's having his leg pulled the whole thing sounds so ridiculous.)

The game is a great source of colorful language. For instance the other day I heard someone described as being one of those guys who was "born on third base and thinks he hit a triple." Now I'm sure my friend who said it didn't come up with that himself so the expression must have some currency, but *I'd* never heard it before and I thought it was brilliant. More than that, I understood it immediately. Do you think a Belgian would have? Or, try explaining that one to an Egyptian.

Baseball is such a well-established metaphor in American life that virtually any baseball term can cross over and make its way in everyday language. But what I love is when a baseball term crosses over into another *sport*, such as when we hear that a football quarterback is going for a home run ball.

As against the possibility that we'll ever run out of baseball terms to use in common language, new ones are constantly being created. When we were young, for instance, did we ever hear of a "walk-off" home run or single? No, I never heard the expression until about ten years ago. And what a great term it is too, so very visual; you can just picture the visiting team walking off the field with their heads hung in the dejection of their sudden defeat.

Another newer baseball expression I love is used when a team needs a rally: "Come on, guys, let's put a crooked number on the board!" In other words, something other than a zero or a one. Great, isn't it?

And finally one last language point: Just in case there's any lingering doubt as to what America's iconic game is. The other day Miranda and I walked past a high school football field, complete with chalked yard markers and goal posts. Miranda referred to it as a "ball field." I had to tell her that even though many other sports are played with balls (football, soccer, golf, tennis, basketball, etc.), a "ball field" is a baseball field – it can be nothing else.

You will perhaps recall my optimism regarding the Yankees in my last letter when they were sitting at 13–10 and things were really starting to come together. Well, it's four days later now and 1) our all-star catcher Jorge Posada is injured and out for at least a couple of weeks, 2) a just-released book about A-Rod is making *new* steroid allegations, and 3) the Yankees have lost four in a row and are now a game under .500 at 13–14.

We arrived here in LA today, visiting Eunice (Miranda's sister) and her husband Jeff. Jeff shares with us the inability to think of baseball as "just a game" and he's promised to get Dodger tickets while we're here.

He's originally from Cleveland but like all intelligent people he made plans to get out of the decaying Rust Bowl as soon as he could spell New York. He has, however, remained rather rabidly loyal to Cleveland's basketball Cavaliers so it didn't surprise me to discover that we'll *not* be going to the Dodger game tonight. No, tonight is game 2 in the Cavaliers-Atlanta Hawks series in the second round of the playoffs. So I *know* what we'll be doing this evening.

See you in Phoenix on Saturday,

t.

9 May 2009 – Gilbert, Arizona

Terry,

It's crazy here. You're flying in today, and you'll be experiencing one of the strangest forms of chaos a baseball team has ever put itself into. It's going to be dark fun.

The Diamondbacks fired their manager yesterday. Bob Melvin is gone. Now this news alone is not crazy. In fact, I have longed for his departure for a good while. For one thing, he never took his pitchers out until after they had allowed so many runs and hits that the game was lost. He was so afraid of what the pitchers would think of him. One time a pitcher scowled and shook his head after Melvin took him out and I know Melvin didn't get any sleep that night and probably vowed never to hurt any player's feelings ever again. No matter how many times it cost the team the game.

And I can tell you there have been many games lost over the past two years because of this inability to take a pitcher out in time. His sensitivity to the pitchers' feelings was off the charts!

My rage at this was heightened one game when the starting pitcher had just allowed his seventh run and the camera panned to Melvin in the dugout. You'll never believe what he was doing. He was applying ChapStick to his lips! Carefully, slowly, even lovingly. To me, that was symbolic of something very negative for the future of this team. Can you picture Casey Stengel applying ChapStick?

And it wasn't only that he waited forever to take a pitcher out. He did it with hitters, too. A young player could go for months hitting .111 before Melvin even whispered about the possibility of sending him back to Triple A farm ball. Back to the farm to learn how to hit. Melvin couldn't make himself do something so hurtful.

Maybe it was because hitting was something Melvin never understood. He never saw the connection between hitting a pitched ball and the success of the team. Somehow in his career that was never made clear to him.

So you can see that when I heard he was fired, I said, "Finally!"

But never did I consider that they would hire anyone other than someone who was a lot tougher. A real old-fashioned baseball guy who knew when to hold 'em and knew when to fold 'em. Someone not afraid of his own players. Someone who could look a pitcher in the eye and say, "You are coming out of this game because we are going to lose it if I leave you in. Have a nice shower."

But no.

No no no. We are going even softer, even less hardcore baseball … we are entering very strange waters now.

Who did we hire? An old fashioned, kick-ass manager not afraid of these kids? Quite the opposite. We hired a kid. He is called Hinch. A Dr. Seuss name! Horton Hired a Hinch! He is 34! Younger than many players. He has never managed, ever. At any level. He has never even coached! (He had been a young "executive" in the organization.)

And A.J. Hinch was not hired not as an interim experiment. Oh no. Why do that? He was given a contract through 2012! In his first game as manager, last night, we lost to the worst team in baseball, the Washington Nationals.

The owners said he was hired because of his "sense of organizational advocacy." Would Billy Martin or Leo Durocher know what that term meant?

Have we lost our minds?

Anyway, it will be good to have you in town. You'll be restoring some sanity to the desert.

S.

12 May 2009 – Salt Lake City, Utah

Terry,

I'm in Salt Lake giving a speech to Enterprise Mentors International, a group of heroic business leaders who give money to impoverished peoples around the world to get them started in their businesses. I love that they do not just WAIT for government grants and bailouts, but rather create their own change in the world and show others how to do the same. They remind me of the Oakland A's, especially the A's that are described so well in Michael Lewis's *Moneyball.* The A's find ways to compete with wealthier teams by using brains and guile and vision. Other teams just throw money at their problems.

In the book I'm reading called *The Yankee Years* by Joe Torre and Tom Verducci they talk about how the Red Sox overtook the Yankees, not with money, but also with brains and superior research. The young owners and executives for the Red Sox did the deep player performance homework that the Yankees weren't doing. The Yankees always thought Steinbrenner's money would be enough. Fascinating stories. I love baseball for the many David and Goliath stories it has every year. How much wit and passion enter into winning. More than any other sport.

I am also in this peaceful city nestled inside surrounding lakes and snow-topped mountains (snow-topped even in May), to lie quietly in my bed and recover from your visit.

Kathy and I both marvel at your energy. And we had such a good time trying to keep up with you. I enjoyed the ball game we saw; the catch we played with real gloves and a major league hardball out on a nice Gilbert diamond; visiting Frank Lloyd Wright's western Taliesen, playing guitars together late into the night; I was wiped out after all that and now I am eight pounds heavier (the restaurants were fun too) and back to my training and diet regimen.

I'll say more about the game we saw together in a day or two. It was a revealing experience.

For now, thanks for the visit, and how upbeat and hilarious you always are. Even at your age. But wait. What am I saying? You are only 64. I read today that Shirley Jones, a Broadway musical and screen and TV actress from our era (way back when) is going to pose nude in an upcoming *Playboy*. And she is 75.

That's like you playing for the Yankees. So the idea of you playing for them becomes less absurd with each passing day. But if I do actually find out one day this year that you have taken the field, I'll know that the Red Sox are still ahead of New York in player evaluation capabilities.

Thanks for coming to see us,
Steve

14 May 2009 – on Delta flight #32 between LA and NYC

Steve & Kathy,

Returning home to New York after a week in the West, typing up my thanks to you both. I had a great time on my two-day whirlwind trip to Phoenix. Your thoughtfulness in putting together the itinerary for my stay in the *fifth* largest metropolitan area in the U.S. coupled with your attention to my every whim while I was there ... well, let me just say that it puts a lot of pressure on Miranda and me in our preparations for your visit here in August.

I am, however, in a bit of a quandary about how to write about the trip for the book. Because I just saw you in Phoenix and we were together and talking (or singing) pretty much every waking moment, there's not a lot to write you about that you don't already know. However, much of the trip was about baseball and it belongs in the book so I've hit on the egotistical solution of simply copying relevant entries from my journal.

5/7 Thursday. NYC–LA

Jeff picks us up at the airport and immediately starts talking about how disappointed he is in Dodger outfielder Manny Ramirez. Last year the Dodgers picked up Manny from the Red Sox with only two months of the season left, just long enough for him to almost single-handedly lift the D's into the playoffs. I thought Manny'd been doing okay this year too so I didn't know what Jeff was talking about. Turns out it was just announced that Manny had tested positive for steroids and the league's suspended him for 50 games. Couldn't happen to a more deserving fellow.

Manny is a truly great hitter and a truly awful human being.

5/8 Friday. LA

We go to Dodger Stadium to see LA take on San Francisco. This is the big rivalry in the NL West – a rivalry that started over 100 years and 3000 miles ago when they were the *Brooklyn* Dodgers and the *New York* Giants. Jeff is wearing a Brooklyn Dodgers baseball cap, showing his full support for a team which ceased to exist six years before he was born.

I have been at Dodger Stadium once before – on October 15, 1977. I watched the Yankees beat the Dodgers 4–2 in what remains the only World Series game I've ever seen in person. Guidry threw a 4-hitter and Reggie had a homer and a double. I was a card-carrying

Detroit Tiger fan at the time and more or less accidentally got the ticket, but maybe it was seeing the Yankees in their glory that day that foreshadowed my conversion to Yankee fan twenty-some years later.

Miranda and Eunice profess interest in the Manny-less game, but seem to show more enthusiasm for cruising the various food concession stands. Though Jeff and I will remember the game as a 3–1 win for the Giants, I suspect Miranda will most remember the garlic French fries.

What I found most striking was how polite and helpful the stadium employees were. It's enough to make New Yorkers vaguely uneasy.

5/9 Saturday. LA–PHNX

Morning plane to Phoenix. While flying I read the Dodger program/magazine I bought at the game last night but didn't have a chance to read.

On the way to the Dodger game yesterday I was explaining to Jeff that during the first few years the Dodgers were in LA they were forced to play in the Los Angeles Coliseum which was designed for football and made a very inadequate baseball stadium. I told him I thought the left field fence was just 251 feet away. This was a number that stuck in my baseball memory and it just came to me though I had no idea if it was the actual distance.

In the Dodger program I read a story about the pennant-winning 1959 team which played in the Coliseum. I'm gratified to see the 251-foot distance highlighted. I wonder what other fascinating baseball nuggets are buried in the unused tunnels of my mine.

Steve and Kathy pick me up at the airport and off we go: lunch at Houston's, Frank Lloyd Wright's Taliesin West, drinks at the FLW-designed Biltmore Hotel, dinner at El Chorro Lodge. With a half-pound burger at lunch and a huge cut of prime rib for dinner I'm already over my annual beef quota.

5/10 Sunday. PHNX.

It's Mother's Day so Kathy's off to breakfast with her mother and brother. Steve and I drive to a nearby park where I do my exercise walk and then we play catch together for perhaps the first time in 40 or 50 years. Steve asks me how long it's been since I've had a baseball in my hand and I remind him of my baseball workouts in Mexico. But when I think about it, he's right. Those workouts are done with a tennis ball; I hadn't thrown a real baseball in more than a year.

Steve wanted us to try the batting cages at the park. You can set the machine to deliver major-league speed 90 mph fastballs and I would have liked to take a few swings, but the cages are closed on Sundays. Perhaps it's for the best; this way I remain certain I would have connected with an endless series of hard line drives.

In the afternoon we go to the Diamondbacks game against the Washington Nationals. Somehow Kathy has managed to score the best seats in the house – maybe the best seats I've ever had at a ballgame. We're sitting four rows behind the D-Backs dugout. (In the new Yankee Stadium with its rapacious management, the same seat would cost $2500! Which is – call me crazy – more than you should have to pay to watch a baseball game.)

Throughout the correspondence for our book and in discussion since I've been here, Steve's been complaining about how the Diamondbacks have a painfully anemic offense. Today they make him a liar. They score 10 runs and get A.J. Hinch his first big league win as a manager. The image that will remain with me occurred during post-game congratulations on the field.

Diamondback catcher, Chris Snyder, made a point of getting the final-out ball from his second baseman and then handing it to Hinch when he came off the field. Hinch stuffed it in his back pocket. It will later appear on his mantle as the final-out ball of his first managerial W. And it was the first thing Snyder thought of after the game was official.

Because it was Mother's Day and there was a tie-in with breast cancer awareness, the players all wore pink armbands. A number of the players used pink bats, too. These, Steve says, are clearly the more sexually self-confident players.

During the game Steve points out that all the players are wearing what look like fuzzy necklaces. Apparently they are some new fad that increases or focuses energy, so obviously one can see they'd be very useful to professional athletes, and now it seems that all the players are wearing them. They contain titanium or some other space age element. I wonder if they're as powerful as the previous fads – like pyramids or crystals? Many ballplayers have attended college.

After the game we go to a restaurant near the stadium started by the rock star Alice Cooper. Appropriately it is called "Alice Cooperstown." Good food, good flat screens with, good company. How can I *not* love a sports bar?

In the morning, while I did my exercise walk, Steve walked backwards. I don't know where he finds these things, but some exercise guru has endorsed this offbeat regimen for I'm not sure what and Steve's on it like a cat on a bird. This same guru claims the exercise also helps you regain lost events and memories from your past. Because I am way open-minded when it comes to wacko concepts, I suspend my skepticism as I see Steve stepping backwards across the park.

Back at Steve's house after dinner, I am reluctantly forced to give up any belief in the loony-tunes theory of walking backwards to bring back memories. Steve and I were singing songs we were teenagers on, from the '50s and early '60s, and at one point I remind him of two singers from the Roulette label of that era. Buddy Knox and Jimmy Bowen. I recall that they each had one, and only one, big hit. We both remember Buddy Knox's "Party Doll," but for the life of us, we cannot remember Jimmy Bowen's hit. I forgive myself this lapse because *I* was walking forward.

After Steve goes to bed, I go on the internet to pick up my e-mails and the fact that Bowen's hit was "I'm Stickin' With You." (Be a great song to use for an Elmer's glue commercial.)

A terrific day.

5/11 Monday. PHNX–LA.

Steve drives me to the airport in the morning and Jeff picks me up in Burbank. Back at Jeff and Eunice's house in East Hollywood, Miranda asks if I can drive her to Von's to pick up some groceries. In Von's trying to find Triscuits, I suddenly become aware of the song being piped through the in-store sound system – "Party Doll."

Ain't life a marvel!

Is any of this interesting? Obviously it's endlessly fascinating to me, but it probably does raise the question whether personal journals should ever be read by anyone whose handwriting is not an exact match for that in the journal. And yet, so many of us keep journals (though it strikes me that most journals today are probably not handwritten, but rather kept on laptops.) I guess when I say "us" I'm talking about writers.

Why is there this journal-keeping need? This desire to record our daily observations and thoughts? Are we really so egotistical that we think these things are important? Or is it rather that later in life we simply don't want people saying, "Why is that old guy in the park walking backwards?"

For me, I think that the answer to both of those last two questions is Yes.

It occurs to me, Steve, that we actually owned records of many of those oldies songs we were singing Sunday evening. So here's a question: what was the *first* record you ever bought? I bring that up because the first record I ever bought has a baseball connection. It was a 45rpm Teresa Brewer song called "I Love Mickey." The Mickey of the title was Mickey Mantle, who actually had a small talking part on the record. And no, we did not sing it on Sunday. Just as well.

I might point out that Kathy was also singing with us on Sunday. I did not mention her in the journal entry because it was a reference to the songs of our youth. For Kathy those songs are history, not nostalgia. This is the cross we bear for marrying women so much younger than we; they have different memories. I'll bet neither Kathy nor Miranda knows the tragic story of Herb Score, just to highlight one instance. There are, however, compensations.

Thanks again for everything,

terry.

15 May 2009 – Gilbert, Arizona

Terry,

You exaggerate! They are ... (our wives) ... not all that much younger than we are. We are not Donald Trumps. In fact, when Kathy read your latest mail she said, "I have a record of Party Doll." How could you? I said. We searched through her old 45s. Not there. "Party Doll" was released in the winter of 1957. Kathy was born in the spring of that same year. Kathy and the record were both released in 1957.

As for my walking backwards, I learned it from Matt Furey. I read some of his fitness books a few years ago, then he read some of my books and we became friends. Matt was a NCAA national champion wrestler and later an international martial arts champion. He lives half the year in China where he finds many of his breakthrough fitness ideas.

The Chinese have been practicing backward walking for thousands of years. You should try it, Terry. Backward walking turns back the clock! In many ways. Your back and lower extremities benefit greatly from it. So does your balance, posture and breathing. And yes, lost memories return.

But you do bump into things every so often. So clear your path first.

⊜

Speaking of the necklaces we saw around the necks of the Diamondbacks, I have just mailed you one! It, too, comes from China. A good friend of mine was over there recently and bought hundreds of them. They have titanium in them. Ballplayers all around the league are wearing them.

Titanium emits energy that controls the flow of bioelectric current. When this current is stabilized, the muscles relax and blood circulation increases, allowing for easier movement and pain relief. Now you and I can wear these necklaces when writing! We'll finish this book long before the season is over.

I really enjoyed your visit and look forward to August in New York.

S

ps- I almost forgot to answer your question! What was the first record I ever bought? This is going to give you goose bumps, especially after hearing "Party Doll" pumped into Von McDaniel's grocery store music system. The first record I ever bought was, "I'm Walkin'" by Ricky Nelson. I almost wrote, "I'm Walkin' Backwards" but I won't. Remember the irrepressible Ricky? On the flip side was "Teenager's Romance."

[Editor's note: In the middle of his "ps" Steve has dropped a reference so obscure that I don't believe I exaggerate when I say that not one person in 10,000 would get it. It is so obscure that, while editing these letters for publication, I was tempted to simply take it out. However, on reflection I decided to leave it in because I think it illustrates the illness that afflicts those of us addicted to this game.

Steve refers to my earlier-mentioned visit to the well-known California supermarket chain Von's. But he calls it "Von McDaniel's grocery store." Von McDaniel was an 18-year-old phenom pitcher who pitched in 17 games for the Cardinals during the 1957 season. In 1958, he pitched in 2 more games. That's it! That was his entire major league career. I might add, he has no connect whatsoever with the Von's supermarket chain.

If you do not know or remember Von McDaniel, you are fully forgiven.

If you do remember him, you are not forgiven for: a) having your mind cluttered with the name of an almost unknown player who disappeared from box scores 52 years ago, and b) having fallen prey to an addiction for which there is no known 12-step antidote. tnh.]

17 May 2009 – NYC, NY

steve,

Today's sports page had a picture of the Mets' recently streaking Gary Sheffield and I noticed he was wearing one of those titanium necklaces. I'll bet he started wearing it five days ago when he was hitting .178. Wearing the necklace he's gone 9 for 18 and his average is up to .270.

Major League Baseball is amazing: they outlaw steroids and yet still allow players to wear those necklaces!?! Where's the logic?

terry.

23 May 2009 – Gilbert, Arizona

Dear Terry,

Adversity means different things to different people. I was watching a Diamondbacks game a couple days ago on TV and some of the young players were being interviewed about the two games that were rained out in two straight days. They talked about how tough it was to miss batting practice and their other normal routines and then have to play a double header. "But this is adversity and we have to learn to deal with adversity."

Then the next day the news came that pitcher Scott Schoeneweis's wife died unexpectedly. She was found on the floor of the master bedroom of the couple's home in Fountain Hills, Arizona, by her 14-year-old daughter. The Schoeneweises have four children. Now *that* I think, for Scott and his family, would qualify as adversity.

Even more so than those little raindrops.

Results of today's autopsy on Gabrielle Schoeneweis, 39, won't be released until the test results come back in 45–90 days, according to an assistant at the medical examiner's office who declined to give her name. The Diamondbacks acquired Schoeneweis from the New York Mets during the off season. And I remember that he came into the game we saw together and you said you remembered him from the Mets.

Prayers to his family.

S.

24 May 2009 – New York, NY

steve.

Yes, I did mention Schoeneweis when he came into the game. Seeing him pitch for the Diamondbacks in that game meant that I've now seen him – in person – pitch for three different teams: the Blue Jays, the Mets and the D-Backs.

Here's a trivia question for you, who holds the current major league record for the most games pitched in by a Jew? Just to eliminate one possible answer I'll tell you that Sandy Koufax is third on the list.

terry.

25 May 2009 – Gilbert, Arizona

Terry,

Baseball fans are often too emotional to be logical or even smart. I count myself as an emotional fan. Look at my hysterical meltdown at the news about the naming of young A.J. Hinch as Diamondbacks manager. I'm beginning to regret my words.

I started to regret my unkind words as you and I watched him manage one of his first games, his first victory, in fact, last Sunday afternoon in Phoenix. Because we were sitting right behind his dugout, we could see his young face looking out there onto the field. He looked so innocent and open. And his assistant coaches would take turns standing next to him and telling him about what was actually going on in the game. I felt for him. Who am I to make fun of him?

Then the more I saw him interviewed and the more I watched him the more I liked him. Sure, he was losing games right and left. But he was making changes and being brave. He even had one of his pitchers get angry at him for taking him out TOO SOON! Now we're talking baseball!

Then came the clincher. Billy Beane said that replacing Bob Melvin with Hinch was a brilliant move. Billy Beane is the genius behind the Oakland A's. He was the hero of *Moneyball,* because it was he who knew how to use statistical analysis and brains to outwit the good-ole-boy money network in baseball. He had turned Oakland into one of the most cost-effective teams in the history of baseball, applying sabermetric principles toward obtaining undervalued players. For example, in 2006 the A's ranked 24th of 30 major league teams in player salaries but had the 3rd-best regular-season record.

Billy Beane for Secretary of the Treasury!

And Beane said the Hinch move was brilliant. So I recant. I'm behind young Hinch now all the way. He's bright and bold. Like Beane himself! Beane even says so! Brains versus greed. I like that as a moral match-up.

Manny Ramirez has been suspended for 50 days because of steroid use. But what would happen if they found out that the reporter who broke the story on steroids had used caffeine and even a little Ritalin to stay up late and write his award-winning piece? Would they take a journalism award away? I'm just wondering. Because somehow I can't see that the use of supplements is as deeply "shameful" as the sportswriters say it is. But I could be wrong about this, too.

I like being wrong. You can learn something when you're wrong. When you're right, you learn nothing.

Love to Miranda,

steve.

28 May 2009 – Yankeetown, USA!

steve.

Miranda wakes me each morning. If she didn't ... well, it's likely I'd sleep until noon each day. She jokes about how hard it is to get me up every morning. But it *is* necessary. Because it's my job to go groggily down to the deli in our building and buy the *Times*. Miranda can have no complaints about this morning. She barely touched me and I was up, dressed and out to get the paper.

You see, I wanted the baseball standings in the sports page to confirm what I already knew from seeing the sports scores from last night:

The Yankees are in first place in the AL-East!

Finally the world is beginning to arrange itself in its proper order. Because there it was:

	W	L	GB
Yankees	27	20	–
Boston	27	20	–
Toronto	27	23	1½

Okay, so we were only tied for first, but there was the added bonus that the Mets were also in first in the NL-East. And compare the Yankees' position *this* morning with just 16 mornings ago when we were in third place 6½ behind the Blue Jays and 5½ behind the hated Red Sox.

And what a sixteen days it's been! The Yankees have gone 12–3 with *four* of those wins coming on walk-off rallies. Mark Teixeira is hitting like a $20,625,000 man, which seems fair because that's what they're paying him for the year. Over the 15 games, he hit 8 homers with 22 RBIs and raised his average from .191 to .275. But he wasn't alone: A-Rod, just back from the disabled list, also added 6 homers including an 11th inning walk-off dinger against Minnesota in that span.

And the pitching has come around too. The winner yesterday was A.J. Burnett, whose ERA had ballooned to 5.28, but who threw 6 scoreless innings, allowing only 3 hits and striking out 7. In looking for clues to his turnaround, I studied a picture of him from last night in the *Times*. In the picture he's wearing – you guessed it – one of those titanium necklaces!

At any rate, it's been a lot of fun the last two weeks and it's the thing I do love about the Yankees. Steinbrenner is willing to spend whatever is necessary to put a strong team on the field each year. I know that if I were in another city I'd hate him *and* the Yankees for that in the way that the Yankees have always been hated. But I live in New York and I love having a team that's always in the pennant race and almost always in the playoffs.

You, on the other hand, only two months into the season can realistically only be saying, "Wait 'til next year!" Your D-Backs are 12 games out of it in the NL-West and your superstar pitcher is injured and watching games on TV for who knows how long. So, Steve, it's time for you to stop being the emotional fan you talked about in your last letter and start following the season with a dispassionate big picture overview.

Me? I've still got something to be irrationally rabid about – we're fightin' for first!

Writing about Teixeira's 20mil and Steinbrenner's willingness to write checks reminds me of the famous story about Babe Ruth, after the 1929 season. The Yankees signing him to a then incredible, $80,000 contract for the following year. At a press conference, Ruth was supposedly asked how he could possibly justify making *more* than the President of the United States, who, at that time was making $75,000 per year.

According to legend, Ruth answered, "I had a better year than he did last year."

This was true. While Ruth was hitting .345, with 46 home runs and 154 RBIs, President Hoover was having the 1929 stock market crash around him.

Well, Steve, things have improved for the President of the United States these days. He (or she) currently receives a salary of $400,000 per year.

Do you know what the *minimum* major league baseball salary is today? By coincidence, the minimum salary is … $400,000.

Meaning that while in 1930 only one player in all of major league baseball made as much as the President of the United States, now *every single player* in the game does. Well, it took some 80 years, but … Justice at last!

t.

May 29th – Phoenix

Terry,

I will not give in to my temptation to list the players in the majors (and minors) who are having a better year than Barack Obama is having … but I would NOT include Chris Young on that list. Because he is the worst starter in the history (my history anyway) of ball. Never mind that he's hitting only .169 right now, he is *even worse* in the clutch!

Put a man on third and he turns to jello at the plate. Horrible to watch. Like a bad comic.

All the Indian tribes in Arizona have given him an Indian name: Throwing Good Money After Bad.

    love to M, s.

3 June 09 – NYC, NY, USA

s.

Miranda's parents have some connections that have never been adequately explained to me – and believe me I've asked. Somehow, once or twice a year, Miranda gets a call from her mother asking if we'd like a couple of tickets to a Mets game or a Yankees game on some specific date. If we don't have anything planned, obviously we take them.

About a week ago, her mother called with an offer of Yankee tickets for the second of June. We got there about an hour and a half early because it was our first chance to see the new Yankee Stadium. And?

Well, it's new. And it's got a sushi stand, which is something I always missed when I was going to ball games as a kid back in the '50s at Briggs Stadium in Detroit; didn't you?

It's actually quite nice, but it has a couple of major flaws for which Steinbrenner greed can be given full credit. The first is that the best seats in the place, field level boxes and reserved seats from first base to third are basically empty. The stadium was packed but the best seats weren't being used. (The guy sitting next to me referred to this barren ring around the infield as "the moat.")

There's no mystery about this. No one is sitting there because the seats haven't been sold. They haven't been sold because they're outrageously priced – some of them were on sale for $2,500. Seems a bit much, doesn't it? Well, obviously it was, because when all of the sportswriters started getting on the team about these empty sections, the Yankees were forced to respond – they cut the price in half. So now you can watch a ballgame in seats as good as the ones Kathy got for us for the D-Backs game in Arizona for only $1,250. A piece.

And what about those people who had already bought tickets at the $2,500 price? Well the Yankee brass, knowing that these early buyers might have their noses a little out of joint, but at the same time, unwilling to return any money that they'd already bought new Armani suits with, hit on the happy solution of simply giving each buyer another ticket for each one that he bought. This made sense because the two-and-a-half grand seats weren't going to be sold anyway. The thing that really gets me is that the Yankees don't seem the slightest bit embarrassed by any of this.

The second flaw is that once the stadium had been designed, a huge Connecticut gambling casino called Mohegan Sun asked if, for a tidy penny, they could put in a members-only club directly in centerfield. Well, the tidy penny had its expected allure for the Yankees and a giant concrete block with a tinted black glass front was plopped right in the center of the bleachers. I'm not sure what's in the black box because we were turned away at the door, not being $750-per-year members. I suppose, however, it holds roulette wheels and craps tables to be used by the true Yankee fans during the seventh inning stretch.

The only problem with the Mohegan Sun facility is that, because of its placement, many people sitting in the leftfield bleachers have an obstructed view of center and right field. When I use the word "obstructed," I mean that you can't see *any* of it. Likewise many seats in the right field bleachers can't see *any* of center or left field. The Yankees came to their rescue, however, by putting up television screens on the Mohegan Sun concrete walls that block the view.

Which means that if you're sitting in the leftfield bleachers and a fly ball goes to right or center field, you can quickly turn your head and follow the rest of the play on … well, basically, television … making you wonder why you didn't simply stay home and watch the whole thing on television.

The stadium cost $1.5 billion to build and several thousand fans *at the game* have to watch it on television.

The game itself, however, was great. Seven good innings pitched by our titanium-energized A.J. Burnett. And 12 runs on 13 hits by the pinstripes. It's what we used to call "a laugher." When Hideki Matsui hit the home run that basically iced the game I wanted to celebrate with some sushi, but the stand was on a different floor so I made do with a hot dog.

    t.

Gilbert AZ. – 5 June 2009

Terry,

Doug Davis pitches for the team tonight. Not good. He is 2–6 this year. I imagine that must be because he has an unbelievably high ERA of 3.63. You can't allow *that many runs* and not lose three fourths of the games you pitch, right? Not for this team.

Two nights ago we lost to the Dodgers. The reason? Why, our pitching staff gave up a run! Lost 1–0.

I got your letter in the mail today; thanks. Especially for the quotes you sent me from Cyril Connolly's *The Unquiet Grave.* I especially liked the one you highlighted for me: "From now on specialize; never again make any concession to the ninety-nine parts of you which are like everybody else at the expense of the one which is unique." That reminds me of the Grateful Dead's Jerry Garcia who said, "You do not merely want to be considered the best of the best. You want to be considered the only ones that do what you do." I take your message.

Speaking of unquiet graves and the grateful dead you know, of course, that Harvey Haddix is dead and has been since 1994. But the Diamondbacks 1–0 loss reminded me of Haddix, the pitcher who could locate his pitches with such a soft touch his nickname was "The Kitten." We could use The Kitten right now.

Especially the Kitten that was pitching for the Pirates against the Braves on May 26, 1959. He not only pitched a perfect game in the first nine innings, he went for three *more* innings of perfect ball. No one has ever had a game like that 12 innings of perfect baseball. Then, in the 13th, Joe Adcock hit a home run and Harvey lost.

Funny thing was, according to an article I just read about that game, Harvey thought he should not have been pitching that night. He was ill. He had a terrible cold and very little strength. He told his manager he'd take a shot at it but to pull him quickly if he didn't hold up. After the game his opposing pitcher Lew Burdette called it the best game he ever saw a pitcher pitch.

That's the kind of pitching this Arizona team is going to repeatedly need if it even has a chance to get to .500, much less make the playoffs. Given the bats we use. Other teams use big cylindrical wooden bats with thick solid bat-heads, and we go to the plate with switches of thistle. It seems.

We like quoting William Butler Yeats in these books, so here:

> I went out to the hazelwood
> Because a fire was in my head
> Cut and peeled a hazel wand
> And hooked a berry to a thread

Cut and peeled a hazel wand. I may shout that at our next hitter who goes down swinging, "Cut and peeled a hazel wand?!?! Use a BAT next time!"

But there's some hope. We play a team called the Padres for the next few days in San Diego. How did they come up with that nickname? Did the naming committee brainstorm it and give itself these parameters: "We want the image of a fat, bald, pale little man in a floppy brown robe. Whatever that would be. How about a padre? A what? A padre, you know, a priest in a mission … it would fit geographically because there were a lot of Spanish missions in the San Diego hills. Perfect! Talk about sending a message that we are not to be messed with."

I think the Diamondback hitters are going to welcome this soft opponent for the next few days.

Steve

8 June 2009 – Detroit, Michigan

dear steve,

I am one of the few people on earth who has any possible reason to visit Detroit. Unfortunately I have many. Like a son, daughter-in-law and two grandsons living here. Like a brother and sister-in-law. Like some old friends. Like overwhelming nostalgia. And like, of course, the Detroit Tigers.

The very first major league baseball game I ever went to was a Tiger game here in Detroit. My grandfather took me and I was 8 years old. I can even remember where we sat (in the lower deck on the third base side, though back under the upper deck overhang). The game was against the Washington Senators. I remember Gil Coan played for the Senators (and I wonder if you even remember Gil Coan) and I remember almost all of the Tigers that would have played in that game.

I remember my father teaching me how to score a baseball game in our first house in Detroit. I must have been 7 or 8. We didn't have a television, but we listened to a Tigers' exhibition game on the radio and together we scored each play. By the end of the game I could do it by myself.

I remember what the 1951 baseball cards looked like for George Kell, Freddie Hutchinson, Vic Wertz and Johnny Groth – Tigers all.

I remember those very good Tiger teams from the early '60s that contended for the pennant against those "damn Yankees." I remember the '68 team that won it all in a 7-game World Series against the Cardinals. And then the '84 team that won it all again!

I raise these memories not for their nostalgic value, but to show that I was a dyed-in-the-wool Tiger fan from the time I was old enough to know who the Tigers were. My *grandfather* was a Tiger fan. My *father* was a Tiger fan; he even wrote two books about the team.

In one of those books, he made the point that, for some reason, a baseball fan will always remain a fan of the team that he first became attached to. No matter where he might later move, or even where his team might move, a true fan remains loyal to his first team.

My brother Chato correctly pointed out that Dad would be turning over in his grave if he knew I'd become – the very worst of all possible things – a Yankee fan. Thank God, I thought, that he was cremated.

The fact is I'm not even sure when exactly I became a Yankee fan. When I was 27 I moved to Toronto and through the 13 years I lived there my Tiger loyalties never wavered. I must have seen two or three Blue Jay-Tiger games a year there and I always rooted for the Tigers.

And then I moved to New York and for fully a dozen years I'd go to Yankee-Tiger games with friends and I'd be the only one rooting for the Tigers.

But somewhere in the midst of the Joe Torre reign I made the switch. I didn't even realize it at the start, but then one day I found myself at a Yankee-Tiger game and I knew that in my heart of hearts I wanted the Yankees to win the game. And that was it.

And yet, still there is guilt. And I never feel that guilt, that betrayal of my roots and of my family tradition more keenly than when I'm back here in Detroit.

You see where I'm going with this, right? I am a man wracked by pain and in desperate need of absolution for my traitorous behavior. Fortunately I know you are the man who can grant me that absolution, for you too grew up with the Tigers, and you too have deserted the Tigers. (And with far less provocation, I might add. I mean the lure of becoming a Yankee fan is estimable … but a Diamondback fan?)

So in two days we're about to disappear to France for two months. And we just felt we had to squeeze in a trip to see the grandsons before we left. And here we are. I've seen Lincoln *[Editor's note: the writer's oldest son. tnh]* and his family; I've seen Chato (who threw a terrific Belmont Stakes party for us the day we arrived); I've seen some old friends; I've wallowed in nostalgia a bit; and … I've seen the Tigers. Fortunately they were not playing the Yankees, so for the afternoon I was able to be a whole-hearted Tiger fan again.

Chato got the whole family tickets for a day game yesterday against the Angels – and a terrific game it was too. Trailing 5–4 in the bottom of the eighth, the Angels' pitchers got wild. The Tigers loaded the bases on walks, scored a run on a throwing error and then got another walk to load them again. With two outs a 25-year-old outfielder named Clete Thomas hit a grand slam and suddenly we had a four run lead … and the game.

Clete is a name that occurs only in baseball. I'm not sure why that is, but it's true.

I stand second to no man in my memories and love of the old Briggs/Tiger Stadium, but I have to say I've been to Comerica Park three times now and it just might be my favorite stadium going. It's got real grass; it's open and airy. In general, just a nice place to watch a ballgame. It seems to have one drawback that wouldn't have occurred to *me*, but was pointed out to me by my youngest grandson.

Early on in the game, Cameron announced that he wanted some cotton candy and he kept looked longingly at the big clouds of them every time a vendor passed. I kept putting him off because he'd already had a hot dog and peanuts and a gigantic soft drink, but I promised him we'd get some later. So later was the seventh inning when we went in search.

We went all over the stadium looking; we even knocked on a closed metal door to a back room where, we'd been told by one of the ushers, the stuff was made. Inside we were informed that they'd *run out of cotton candy* in the fifth inning. Cameron, my grandson who is six, told me he thought it was very bad planning on the part of Comerica Park. I had to agree.

He settled for a plastic baseball cap filled with soft ice cream and some horrid-looking, multi-colored sprinkle things all over it.

T.

9 June 2009 – Gilbert, AZ.

Terry,

LOL. I mean, I spilled my coffee when I read what you wrote about your beloved (cremated) father. OMG! That was funny.

I forgive you, now and forever (and officially as no one else can). I believe there is a concept that rises above "lifelong fan loyalty" and that is this: **hometown boys.**

Walking the streets of New York, going to the bars, riding the subway, everyone's talking about the hometown boys. The Yankees play for you if you live there. You aren't going to honor them back? Jeter flies into the stands to catch a foul ball for you, emerges with a bloody face (and the ball in his glove) and you won't cheer him? You won't pull for him to win? Come on!

Our Diamondbacks started playing here after I'd lived here for more than 25 years. They started fresh. No history. A brand new team rising like a phoenix from nowhere, right here in Phoenix …

Who was I not to show up at the park and cheer them on?

They were a bad expansion team, but they got good real fast and even rose up and beat the Yankees in the World Series. I was with them all the way. Because they were my boys.

The other day I noticed that Dan Haren and I were shopping in the same store. He is an amazingly good pitcher for us. What am I going to do, walk over with a Tigers hat on and tell him I'm a Tigers fan? I think not. He works for me now.

He toils on the mound and goes the extra mile on my behalf. I cheer him from the stands sometimes and I can almost see him glancing over and giving me a slight nod. Maybe he hears me. He's reaching back to get this guy out for me.

I forgive you. In fact, there is nothing to forgive. Yankee Stadium is your house now. I can even picture you and Miranda yelling at the Tigers on the field who are trying to win a comeback victory with Rivera walking in from the bullpen to squelch their rally. What are you yelling at the Tigers? This:

"NOT IN OUR HOUSE!"

steve.

12 June 2009 – Paris, France

s.

I arrived in Europe to great disappointment. Not with Paris; Paris never disappoints me, even when it's gloomy, as it is today, it's still wonderful. No the disappointment came when I bought the *International Herald Tribune* and looked at the sports page: Yankees 5, Boston 6. These two words and two numbers were the *complete* coverage of the game in the IHT. This was yesterday.

Today I manage to get on the internet (very complicated) and find that the Yankees have now lost again in the third game in the Boston series. This means we are now 0–8 against the Red Sox this year. Given that, I suppose I should feel grateful that we're only 2 games behind them in the AL East.

I am afraid that for the first time I will *not* be buying the *Herald Tribune* each day while I'm in Europe. I have spent close to 2000 days of my life on the continent and on virtually every one of those days (except for Sundays when the paper doesn't publish) I've bought the paper. However sensible a decision this is, it's still a sad one for me.

A part of it is due to "Yankees 5, Boston 6." I mean it's really not that much information, is it? Another part comes from the cost, which is now 2.5 Euros, or about $3.50 in U.S. dollars. But the clincher is, of course, that everything I'd want to know from the IHT is on the internet and, in the case of baseball scores, it's not only a lot more timely, but also in much more detail. As anyone will be quick to point out, this is progress.

As you know, I consider myself comfortable with change and do not see myself as a man longing for bygone "better" days. But I do occasionally find myself susceptible to a keen bout of nostalgia. My IHT decision brings on one of these bouts.

From the very first time I ever visited Europe in 1973, the *Herald-Tribune* has been a sacred piece of the experience. Back then it was virtually the only English language paper available in non-English speaking countries, and it was certainly the only place to find out news about American sports, especially baseball. This news was much abbreviated, of course, but at least you could get a 20–30 word summary and a line score of the ball games.

Also, because of the time difference, the IHT baseball coverage was two days late. In the case of a Friday game, you wouldn't find the result until Monday, there being no Sunday paper. I remember in 1983 being in Paris on my own and following the World Series in the IHT. I was reading the coverage in the paper one day and wondering whether the Phillies might be able to win the Series when it occurred to me that it was already over. I just didn't know the outcome. And, short of making a transcontinental phone call, I wouldn't find out until the next day. Today, of course, I could just pop into an internet café and check espn.com.

My fondest (and most *Twilight Zone*-ish) memory of the IHT was in 1988 on a road trip through the Loire valley with my sons. The trip was very important to me because my father had died just a few months earlier and here I was with my sons establishing the kind of memories that they would have of me after *I* died. One morning having coffee at the B&B where we were staying, I was reading the IHT sports page and there was a small filler at the bottom of the page – a humorous quote about watching a ball game at Yankee Stadium taken from one of my father's books! It was the most eerie coincidence of my life; it was as if he were talking to me from the grave.

Well, if he wants to say anything to me today, he better make sure it gets on the internet, because if it's in the IHT, I'm gonna miss it.

t.

13 June 2009 – Gilbert Arizona

Terry,

Kathy says I should stop watching these baseball games on TV. For my own good. She says I am never angry or upset in regular life, but turn on a Diamondbacks game and she sees what she calls my "dark side" come out.

Yes, I yell at the screen. And I add sarcastic commentary to the game. A few days ago I watched a game that lasted nearly six hours. It went 18 innings. We were up 6–1 in the 9th, looking like everything was in hand. But then our young manager who has never managed or coached sent our "closer" in to close the game except that he hasn't been much of a closer, having allowed 16 runs in his last 14 innings. But the manager has stayed with him. Doesn't want to hurt his feelings by demoting him. Oh sure, you lose a few games in the process of proving you're a real "player's manager" (you care more about the players moods than you do about winning or losing). So this closer, who really isn't a closer, comes in and I hide my head in my hands. We traded Val Verde our real closer and decided to try this guy Qualls at closer this year. And he comes in and allows the Padres (soft team, fat-bald-guy-in-a-loose-robe-mascot Padres) to score five runs in the ninth!!!!!! We have to go into extra innings!

And in these extra innings our manager orders a very strange bunt at one point, a bunt that made no sense, with runners at first and third and a guy at the plate who has been hitting over .500 with runners in scoring position. Even Mark Grace the color commentator, usually quite a home team advocate, said the bunt was puzzling, as strategy. I was yelling at the TV screen. Demanding an explanation!

Kathy thinks this watching of TV baseball is not good for me. My well-being, overall, as a human, psychologically speaking, may be, in her eyes, threatened by this ball club. My brother had a heart attack recently from stress. And he's even younger than I am.

And anyway we won. In 18 innings. They, the Padres, ran out of pitchers and had to put in a shortstop to pitch and our boys finally found someone in this league that they could hit. We won! What does bipolar mean exactly? Up and down up and down? Manic one inning, depressed the next?

I've been noticing something ominous that may prove Kathy to be right. You were in advertising so you will know what I'm talking about. *Targeted* media buys. Marketing to niche audiences. Sound familiar? On the Diamondbacks TV channel during the games there are more and more pharmaceutical ads! Truly. For depression, for social anxiety, and for bipolar disorder. The drug companies have found their perfect target audience. Diamondback fans. We are developing all the symptoms they talk about in these ads!

I don't know. Maybe I'll back off a bit in the TV department. Maybe I'll just watch the national game of the week. Try to become a fan of baseball itself. Instead of following this team. Baseball itself is quite a good thing. This I know is true.

love to Miranda,   s.

15 June 2009 – Paris

Steve,

Please give it up. The Diamondbacks chances, I mean. They're out of it! Wean yourself from your earlier hopes for a D-Back playoff appearance this year. To continue this vain wish, as Kathy points out, is madness at best and a heart attack at worst.

To quote you: "Baseball itself is quite a good thing." Write that sentence out and post it in key locations in your world – next to the TV where you watch games; near your dining room table where you read newspaper accounts of the D-Back games the mornings after; on the dashboard of your car where you might be listening to a game on the radio.

After that, you must develop the mindset I was urging on you before: become the dispassionate, and yet incisive, observer of the game. It's a valid role, and a much saner one than being a D-Back fan. This is actually kind of an interesting season, with a number of storylines (as journalists seem to call them these days) worthy of your attention and sage analysis. Let me suggest a few:

1) Three teams this year seem to have adopted the strategy of trying to win their division with only one pitcher. I cite the Blue Jays, the Royals and the Mets. The strategy seems suspect to me, and this is in no way to slight the three pitchers these teams are relying on – Halladay, Greinke and Santana. In fact, I will boldly predict that each of them will win 20 this year (this, a rarity in an era when some years *no* pitcher in the majors wins 20). But in the end, as in-depth students of math will tell you, 20 is *not* 86, which is pretty much the minimum number of games a team needs to win to capture a division title. Somewhere you've got to dig up 66 more wins.

2) Nolan Ryan, the former iron-man pitching great and now general manager of the Texas Rangers, has openly questioned the current belief that pitchers are fragile athletes with glass arms that are certain to shatter if they're forced to throw 101 pitches on any given day. It wasn't many years ago that top pitchers would throw 20–30 complete games in a season and start every fourth day.

What Ryan wants to do is get the Ranger starters strong enough that they can go deep into ball games on a regular basis. He doesn't believe this will hurt their performance and it means the team will be able to carry fewer pitchers on the roster, thus giving his manager added in-game strategic flexibility with more position players.

So what's the problem? Well, I heard a couple of ESPN announcers suggesting that it was a risky approach that might ruin pitcher's arms and shorten their careers. Where, I wonder, is the evidence for this? Surely there must be a computer run someone could set up that would tell us whether pitchers from the '50s, '60s and '70s had more injuries than today's coddled twirlers. Or if their careers were noticeably shorter.

I'd like to see this analysis done because I honestly don't trust my memory ... which tells me there wasn't any real difference. Maybe there was. But right now all the arguments seem very anecdotal.

3) The success of the Dodgers this season is also fun to watch. Mainly, I guess, because I love Joe Torre and think he got a raw deal from the Yankees. It was great to see him succeed like he did last year, sneaking the Dodgers into the playoffs, while the Yankees with their quarter billion dollar payroll watched the games on television.

Then this season, he's sitting in first place with his team having the best record in the majors. And they've accomplished all of this while their superstar offensive player is sitting out a 50 game suspension. Now, no matter what you think of Manny (and he's not someone I'd have on a shortlist of potential godfathers for any offspring of mine), it's impossible to argue that the Dodgers aren't a stronger team when he's in the line-up. And yet they're holding up just fine without him for the time being.

4) And just to give you one more storyline to draw your attention from your failed Diamondbacks, let me give you Ichiro Suzuki. I was made aware of him before he ever played a major league game in 2001 and I've followed his brilliant career ever since.

Back then I was living in Paris and was taking a conversational French course with a bunch of 20-something foreign students. I was generally the oldest person in the class by two decades or more. There were Italians and Mexicans, Argentineans, Chinese, Israeli, Turkish and English and students from many other countries; we had lots of fun together. There was one Japanese kid named Makio whom I became friends with and who was a big baseball fan. He told me there was a Japanese player coming to play for Seattle that year and that he was going to be a sensation.

I told him he was crazy, that no player could jump from Japanese baseball to the majors and make a stir, especially in his first season. He assured me that Ichiro was going to set the league on fire. What makes you think so, I asked.

"Because he's a genius!" Makio replied.

In the end, I bet Makio that Ichiro wouldn't hit .300. Of course, by the end of the year, I looked like a total fool. Ichiro won the American League batting championship, hitting .350; stole 56 bases; won a Gold Glove for his play in right field; won the Rookie of the Year award and capped it off by being named MVP. I lost my bet.

But to really see something very special, watch him hit a few times. He sometimes takes a full swing, but just as often he'll bunt or just slap at the ball in a way that makes you suspect a possible reincarnation of Wee Willie Keeler. The only knock against him is that he doesn't get a lot of walks. But on the other hand he rarely strikes out. The guy's a genius in the batter's box!

So here's the story about this year, Ichiro's ninth season. In each of his first eight seasons he's collected more than 200 hits. This year an injury kept him out the first 9 games of the season and I feared for his streak. But since he's been back he's making up for lost time. Right now he's hitting .360 and has 87 hits. Yes, I know that's a long way from 200, but this is an accomplishment that takes a whole season to reach and he's on a pace to make it right now. Keep an eye on him and away from your 2-runs-a-game Diamondback offense; you'll live longer.

Just looking out for your health,

terry

16 June 2009 – Carmel, California

Dear Terry,

One of the great things about being in Carmel by the sea is that we do not have to watch the Diamondbacks on TV as they fall over 15 games behind the Dodgers (as they have), but we can, instead, enjoy the Pacific Ocean and out-of-town newspapers. Sweet misty relief.

Your letter from Paris on the *International Tribune* was poignant. I had a similar experience. In the airport in Monterey I bought a *New York Times* on a whim thinking I could read some first-hand accounts of how your Yankees were doing and much to my delight I saw a little photo teaser of A-Rod in a box. But when I got on the plane and turned to the box wondering which page the Yankee story it referred to was on I saw to my disappointment that the box was referring me to the *NY Times* website! No stories at all today in the paper itself about baseball.

Must be a west coast edition? Whatever. No wonder the internet rules. It rules because it rules.

You had counseled me in an earlier correspondence in an earlier book not to long for the good old days. Things today are better than ever. Really true. Take *The Taking of Pelham 123*. We saw that new movie in a theater as soon as we got home and one of my first thoughts is that it was much better than the original. Great editing, great subway shots, great pacing, great dialogue, great music ... everything better. (You'll recall that they filmed part of that movie in the hotel where Kathy and I stayed in NY while we were last visiting you and that we saw Denzel Washington and John Travolta shooting scenes at our hotel.)

On your visit here you told me you had just read *Baseball Joe at Yale* (Copyright 1913), a book I sent you just prior to our starting this book. Because I remembered reading that book in 1954 when it was in the library in Birmingham where you and I grew up. A year or two later you yourself wrote a short story about a black basketball player at the University of Texas. I marveled at how good that story was. And so for some reason I was just considering reading Philip Roth's novel about baseball called *The Great American Novel*. Fictional storytelling is maybe the best medium, above and beyond TV baseball, newspaper's diminishing accounts and live viewing. It may be what I turn to exclusively now. To preserve my mental well-being.

. In the same *NY Times*, after not finding anything in the sports section worth reading I noticed an article by Colum McCann about James Joyce. In it he quotes Vladimir Nabokov as saying that the purpose of storytelling is "to portray ordinary objects as they will be reflected in the kindly mirrors of future times; to find in the objects around us the fragrant tenderness that only posterity will discern and appreciate in far-off times when every trifle of our plain everyday life will become exquisite and festive in its own right: the times when a man who might put on the most ordinary jacket of today will be dressed up for an elegant masquerade."

That sounds so much better than reality right now. Love to M,
S.

17 June 2009 – Paris, France

Steve,

Knowing that a remake of *The Taking of Pelham 123* was about to be released, I made a point of watching the original on DVD a few weeks ago. I had never seen it before because it came out during my Missing Film Decade (1966–1976).

Because we had little money and two kids who needed babysitting, Trudi *[Editor's note: Trudi was my first wife and mother of my two sons. tnh]* and I almost never went to a movie during those years. It was too great an expense. Okay, I lied a bit. During that decade I *did* see a number of films, but none of those films had characters played by actors, instead they had all been drawn by Walt Disney.

So I finally saw *The Taking of Pelham* and really very much liked it. Why did I see the old Walter Matthau version instead of waiting a few weeks for the Denzel version? Because, unlike you, I don't trust remakes.

One of my favorite films of all time is *Charade* (1963) with Cary Grant and Audrey Hepburn. (I love it for a number of reasons, one of which is that it takes place in one of my favorite cities – the one I'm in right now.) In 2002, Hollywood decided to remake it and, for reasons unclear to me (embarrassment with the final product?) they changed the name to *The Truth About Charlie*. And the truth is, it's a dreadful film.

And that's just one example – though a particularly flagrant one, I think – of the folly of remakes. Having said that I must admit I'm quite looking forward to seeing the new *Pelham 123*; because not only you, but also the *New York Times*, have had good things to say about it. And you *know* what a slave I am to the *Times*.

You also mention in your last e-mail the book *Baseball Joe at Yale*. I very much want to write about the book, which I finished some time ago, but I'm going to hold off on that until I get back to New York because there are a number of bits I'd like to quote and my copy of the book's in the Apple.

But in the meantime, what's your favorite baseball book? I'll send you a list of my top ten after you reply. (But, just as a little preview, I might mention that, a] *Baseball Joe* doesn't make the list – sorry – and, b] you were the editor of one of my ten.)

There were a number of other interesting things I wanted to mention about that Harvey Haddix "perfect game" that you wrote about a while back.

Do you know that until 1991 that game was considered a no-hitter and then major league baseball changed the definition of what a no-hitter was and Haddix's game, along with a number of other pitching gems, was removed from the list? You said Haddix died in 1994. Maybe it was the disappointment of this retro-demotion after 32 years of thinking he'd pitched a no-hitter that hastened his demise.

You also said Joe Adcock won the game with a "home run" in the 13th. Well, he hit the ball out of the park all right, but in circling the bases he passed the runner immediately in front of him and was actually only given credit for a double.

And finally, Haddix was not called "The Kitten" because of his pitching style, but rather because the team thought he looked like a pocket version of the team's star starting pitcher at the time, Harry Brecheen, whose nickname, you'll recall, was "The Cat."

On the subject of no-hitters, have you ever seen one? In person?

A more interesting question is: have I? I'm asking you that question because I want you to answer it for me. I'm unable to myself. Here's what happened:

In mid-August of 1965 I was in Chicago visiting Trudi's family (we weren't married until later in the year). I mentioned that I'd love to see a ballgame in Wrigley Field and Trudi suggested we pick a game and go. So on the day, we were riding the el to the game when I noticed a guy on the car with us listening to a transistor radio. It seemed to be a baseball game and I assumed it must be the White Sox playing in an earlier time zone because the Cubs' game wasn't due to start for another hour or so. Being chatty, I asked the guy what the score was.

"No score," he said, "but it's only the second."

"Who's pitching?"

"Larry Jackson."

This last answer made no sense, because Jackson was supposed to be pitching for the Cubs that day in the game we were going to see – the game that wouldn't start for an hour. Well, in fact, that *was* the game we were supposed to see.

The day before, there had been a bad storm in Chicago and the Cubs had been rained out. To make up for it, they scheduled a double-header for today. In those days, you will recall, Wrigley Field didn't have lights so all their games were day games. In order to protect against the possibility of the second game having to be called because of darkness, the Cubs moved back the start time of the first game. It was undoubtedly in the newspapers, but somehow we'd missed it.

When we finally got to the game, it was in the fourth inning and the score was still 0–0, a real pitchers' duel. Jackson versus Jim Maloney for the Cincinnati Reds. Maloney didn't really have his control so the Cubs always seemed to have men in scoring position but just couldn't manage to push across a run. Because of our late arrival and all the runners the Cubs had, it wasn't until the sixth inning that I looked at the scoreboard and realized that Maloney hadn't yet allowed a hit.

At the end of nine, the score was still 0–0 and Maloney had pitched a no-hitter! It was all very exciting and throughout I was trying to explain to Trudi what was going on and how rare this was. In the end, Maloney pitched a 10-inning no-hitter and Cincinnati won the game 1–0. I don't have the box score, but in my memory (which I know is not to be trusted on this) Maloney walked the bases loaded twice during the game and wound up with 9 or 10 walks in the game. We then stayed for the second game which was not nearly as exciting.

So, did I see a no-hitter? Does watching the last 6 innings of a 10-inning no-hitter count as "seeing a no-hitter?" Or do you have to see the whole thing? I will accept your answer without question. But it's only fair to warn you that even if you pronounce that I've *not* seen a no-hitter in person, I'll still be telling this story to my grandchildren and, I hope, great grandchildren until they're bored stiff. Much as, I suspect, Harvey Haddix told the story of his "perfect game" until the day he died.

From Paris, France, this is Terry Hill … good night.

t.

18 June 09 – Gilbert, Arizona

Terry,

You are in Paris, so you are really in the arms of tradition. I, on the other hand, am in Phoenix. So I am not. In fact, the Arizona Diamondbacks, who won the World Series wearing black and purple, are now a team that wears red!

Tradition means nothing here.

You love the tradition of the original movie, rather than the sequel. You like to be a stickler about how Harvey Haddix really got his name The Kitten.

I, on the other hand, like imagined stories. In fact, I so like stories that I have just finished a book of fiction, a mystery. It will be the first of a 12 book series, (book two already started).

So I'm going to continue with my story of why perfect Harvey was called the Kitten. I like it better. That he gently placed his pitches, like a kitten's paw might place a toy mouse, in the spots where hitters could not hit them.

S.

19.VI.09 – Paris

s.

Today, I received messages from two friends, each announcing that he'd just finished a novel. You, and my friend Jordi Punti in Barcelona. His, I have to say, is probably the greater accomplishment because it's in Catalan and it took him 5½ years to finish. For me, anyway, and I suspect for you, it would be much harder to write a novel in Catalan than English. *Ne c'est pas?*

On the other hand, I don't read Catalan so I'll probably read yours first.

Let me just add two last things to the no-hitter discussion, then, I promise, I'll drop the subject:

The first time I became aware of no-hitters was probably the first year I really started following baseball – 1952. That year Virgil Trucks for my Tigers pitched *two* no-hitters. Amazing! Especially since his overall record that year was 5–19 and the Tigers finished last in the American League for the very first time in their history. He won each by a 1–0 score.

The strangest no-hitter, I think, was a combined no-hitter for Ernie Shore and Babe Ruth in 1917. You might even consider it for "perfect game" status for Shore. Ruth, who was a pitcher for the Red Sox then, started the game and walked the first batter on four pitches. The Babe, however, didn't think he'd thrown four balls and argued vehemently with the umpire. In fact, he tried to physically attack the umpire with a predictable result – he was thrown out of the game.

Ernie Shore came in to replace Ruth and on his first pitch the runner on first tried to steal second and was thrown out. Shore then retired 26 straight batters.

In the record books, it's a "combined no-hitter," but it seems a bit of a gift to give Ruth shared credit; after all, he didn't manage a single out.

    t.

21 June 2009 – Paris.

s.

Yesterday, I got caught up in running errands and cruising art galleries on the Left Bank and by the time we got back, it was really too late to go to the internet café. As a result, it marked the first day this season that I had no idea how the Yankees had done the day before.

Today, I know: they lost. But fortunately they won yesterday. Not that that does much for them, they still trail the Red Sox by 3 games. That's three games I doubt they'll make up unless A-Rod comes to life at some point. Girardi sat him on the bench in yesterday's win. "Fatigue" was given as the reason, but there were cynics who suggested that the man's batting average being a smaller number than his weight was possibly a more important factor in the decision.

Tonight is a big night in Paris – Fete de la Musique. Starting at 7 in the evening in more than a hundred locations all over the city, musicians put on free concerts. There's rock, techno, folk, salsa, classical, gospel, jazz, klezmer, blues, hip-hop, operatic, rap … virtually everything but country which hasn't really made it over here yet.

There's an overall official schedule which is in all the newspapers, but some of the best concerts are the ones chipped in by small cafes that simply offer singers or bands a stage for the evening. We're going to start at 9 at Place du Marche Ste-Catherine where we'll have dinner at an outdoor café and listen to reggae. From there we'll walk back to our apartment and stop at whatever sounds interesting.

It really is a fabulous event. You'd love it. The music continues to 4 or 5 o'clock, but I'll be in bed long before that – after all, I've got to get up in the morning to check the Yankee score.

au revoir,

t.

Gilbert, Arizona – 24 June 2009

Dear Terry,

We, Kathy and I, noticed when you visited us here that you had tremendous reservoirs of energy, especially for an older gentleman. And the reader should realize you are older than I.

By a few months.

And now you say they have sat A-Rodriguez down on the bench – taken him out of the starting lineup, because of fatigue. It's baseball.

How could there be fatigue? Have you ever watched a game? Especially a third baseman's game? I've played that position. When you and I were young. You played short and I was on third. No fatigue. Lots of anticipation, and a few key plays, but fatigue?

But let's just say there is fatigue. I kind of got sidetracked there and almost missed making my point. My point is that *you* could play. You could step in and play third base for A-Rod until he got his energy back to the level of yours.

And I'm not kidding. I know you were joking earlier when you kept talking about playing this year for the Yankees. But one of the things I love about baseball is that *you* really *could* play. Some innings no balls would come to you. How hard would that be? And some grounders you would field and throw to first. And the runner would be OUT! Seriously. What other sport can say that?

You'd never joke about playing football for the Jets. Because we both know that one play, *one play* and it would be a stopping of the game for the paramedics to clear the field. Of you!

You'd be carried out.

And pro basketball? Forget it. Ten seconds on the floor for the Knicks at Madison Square Garden, and the fans would be roaring at you ... at how you couldn't keep up, how your every shot would be blocked, every dribble stolen and every pass intercepted.

But baseball! You could play! That's why the game is so wonderful.

But here's the paradox! It actually takes more skill to play baseball than any other sport. Danny Ainge found that out. So did Michael Jordan. Baseball requires the most elaborate skills of all to play at the major league level. And please notice that I said skill and not talent. Skill! There's a big difference. Oh, it's huge and I'm going to talk about that in a week or so ... I've got a bunch of notes on that subject saved up to unload on you while you are sipping wine and eating quiche in Paris and trying to follow the Yankees.

I wish I too was in a foreign land and could not get my team's results. We are now 17 games out of first. We joked about it when it was12 but it's 17 now.

Yet baseball itself is still great. Kathy and I watched two amazing fielding plays last night by our shortstop Stephen Drew and our first baseman Mark Reynolds (he was playing third when you saw him). Yes we beat the Texas Rangers and what a pretty sight those plays were!

So forget the season. Just enjoy one game at a time. That's my new approach. Living in the present. Not obsessing about the past or the future. The present is the best place for this team to be. The past and the future are both too painful. Please don't mention either one of them when you write.

love to M, steve.

28 June 2009 – Los Angeles, California

Dear Terry,

I had enough hotel miles accumulated in my travels for Kathy and me to be staying here for free at the Beverly Hilton lounging out by the pool seeing all the Dodger blue caps worn by starlets. Or maybe not starlets but just young women who have a kind of Beverly Hills look (versus the usual tanks of obesity you see back home powering through the discount food stores with their carts piled high with extra carbohydrates).

The news here in LA is twofold, first: Michael Jackson has just died. He was the opposite of an obesity tank. Papers said they had to force him to eat anything at all any given day. And the drugs he was taking into that frail body were pretty overwhelming. Almost life-threatening, his doctors conceded, staring down at his corpse.

We went to his house.

It was part of a little tour we took in a van that left from the hotel in the morning and took us through Beverly Hills and surrounding homes. I wanted to see where Joe DiMaggio and Marilyn lived, and we saw that nice house. They took us to Michael's house on the way back and it was surrounded with flowers, media trucks and happy mourners with cameras.

⊗

Second, Manny Ramirez is back from drug suspension this week, so the papers are covering that, and how no one in LA cares that he took a steroid or two. A human growth pill. Maybe just half a pill, who cares? He's back. Not that the Dodgers even need him, they are doing so well under Joe Torre.

I'm out by the pool here with a baseball magazine I brought with me and there was an article about a baseball player named Bryce Harper who they say is the best player in the nation. Even though he's only 16. His statistics are awesome. He is a catcher, but when he takes the mound he can fire the ball in at 96mph. And he illustrates what I love about baseball.

What I love about baseball is its relationship to practice. In the past half year, because of my job (which is to coach people and train corporate teams to perform more effectively) I have read three books about the myth of talent and the reality of practice. These were all very good books, and I highly recommend them, especially to people who believe in talent as a determining factor in one's success. That's a myth.

The books were: *The Outliers* by Malcom Gladwell, *Talent is Overrated* by Geoff Colvin, and *The Talent Code* by Daniel Coyle. All three books reveal, through dramatic research, that people we thought possessed inherent talent had actually practiced their craft in deeper and more meaningful ways. Even the Beatles! Who had put in more band hours than any band of their time at the outset due to an amazing string of 8-hour gigs in Hamburg.

Back to that 16-year-old baseball player. How did he get so good that the majors already want him at age 16? (Good news for you: his goals include being "in pinstripes" ... we all know what that means ... other goals: to be in the hall of fame, and to be considered the greatest baseball player who ever lived.)

Bryce was playing tee-ball at age three. Practicing hard. At age three. He has played between 80 and 130 baseball games a year for the past seven years...from when he was age 8 to age 16. Most kids that age play about a fifth of that. And here is the key to everything right here: his dad has been his lifelong hitting coach. Spending day and night with young Bryce, on the field and in the cage, pitching him sunflower seeds, bottle tops and dried red beans.

That's it right there. All three books that show how practice trumps talent. They give special tribute to unusual, creative, obsessive types of practice. Like firing dried red beans at your son. And challenging him to hit them. So that when he plays in a game and sees an actual baseball coming in at him it looks like a beach ball in slow motion. Which field will I choose to hit it to?

So if you study baseball long enough, you can learn how to succeed at anything.

love to Miranda, S.

July 10, 2009 – Lyon, France

steve,

We're here in Lyon staying in a neighborhood called Croix-Rousse. This is the old silk-weaving district that sprung up in the early 1800s after the invention of the Jacquard loom by, coincidentally enough, a guy named Jacquard – Joseph-Marie Jacquard.

Lyon had for centuries been the silk capital of Europe and the Jacquard loom was a revolution in the industry. The only problem was that the new looms were too big for the buildings in Old Lyon so a whole new complex was built in a previously sleepy little adjunct to the city called Croix-Rousse.

The new buildings all had very high ceilings with big tall windows and wooden beams to accommodate the looms, and for more than a century business boomed. But then – well, I don't suppose I have to tell you what happened next because it's pretty much general knowledge – the devastation of the silkworm disease! That and the development of synthetic fabrics pretty much wiped out the silk business.

So now you've got this whole neighborhood of high-ceilinged, big-windowed, wooden-beamed, but basically unused buildings. Does the word "lofts" come to mind? Well that's basically what happened; the real estate industry took the baton from the silk industry and Croix-Rousse became a hot address. Today, the area is considered, in French, "Bo-Bo" (*bourgeois-bohemes*), which means it's basically for well-off, artistic types. So obviously I fit right in, except for the "well-off" part.

So here we are living for a month in Croix-Rousse on rue Jacquard. We're in a very nice large apartment which has, as not the least of its charms, internet access! This is a long way of getting around to: baseball. Which, with the aid of the internet, I am now free to be obsessed with again.

I must admit I was feeling very guilty about the Yankees this past month. I mean when I boarded that plane to Paris back on June 10th, the Yankees were in first place. Somehow my leaving NYC upset some celestial alignment or knocked the balance of baseball's weights and measures wonky or screwed up some delicate karma. The result was that from a series of Parisian internet cafés I could only watch helplessly as the team foundered (now that's a verb I do not often use, but the situation was grave and extreme verbs are needed). They fell as much as four games back.

I still feel that for the good of the team I should return to New York, but somehow my move to Lyon has turned things around and this morning as I check the scores, I see the Yankees are in first place again! Tied with Boston at 51–34. The alignment has been adjusted.

Miranda suggests that this is all silly and mindless, this belief that somehow my movements affect the Yankees' fortunes. Plus she pretty much laughed in my face when I proposed cutting our stay in France short and going back to New York to turn the team around.

You know me, Steve. You know that I am *not* a superstitious guy. Quite the opposite. I don't believe any of that spirituality stuff, or rabbits' feet or horseshoes or psychology or four-leaf clovers or any other of those made-up fables. But it seems scientifically pretty obvious to me that if the Yankees were in first when I left New York, fell to four back when I was in Paris ... well, *duh*. You know something is happening here but you don't know what it is – do you, Mr. Jones?

I might just add that the Mariners' genius at the plate, Ichiro Suzuki, got 3 hits last night to give him 123 for the season. He needs 77 more and there are 77 more Mariners games. Barring injury ... well, I'd cross my fingers, but I'm not superstitious.

My best to Kathy, who undoubtedly understands far better than either of us what a jacquard loom might be able to produce,

t.

11:33 pm – July 13, 2009 – Lyon, France

s.

18 years ago, today, in a restaurant at 88 University Place in Manhattan, there was a wedding. You were the best man and I, the groom. Miranda and I celebrated our anniversary by going out to dinner at a Berber restaurant. (What's *your* favorite Berber place, Steve?)

Miranda didn't think the food was so great, but we really went there for the view. The restaurant is on the edge of the high plateau where Croix-Rousse is located, and as a result, has a beautiful long view of the rest of Lyon spread out below. This was important tonight because at 10:30 there were fireworks all over town in anticipation of Bastille Day tomorrow. It was quite a show.

I bring up all this history because of the contemplative mood brought on by these special days. I speak, of course, of the special three days of the All-Star break. This is the traditional "halftime" of the baseball season. Days for looking back ... and looking forward:

Three days ago I was certain the Yankees were on their way –
that my move to Lyon had righted the universe and it was now clear-
sailing to the World Series. Over the next three days they looked like
the worst team in baseball, losing 3 straight to the Angels. Over the
same three days, the Red Sox were *winning* 3 straight over the Royals.
So at the break we're 3 games back.

I again tried to convince Miranda that we might want to think about
getting back to New York ahead of schedule, this time suggesting that
it was necessary to turn around the fortunes of her Mets, who've gone
from 2nd place 2 games behind the Phillies to 4th! place 6½ back since
we've been away.

This tack was greeted by pretty much the same laughter as my
earlier let's-help-the-Yanks approach. Miranda suggested that maybe
the Mets' 11–20 record since we departed was due more to the fact
three star position players (Reyes, Delgado & Beltran) and their second
best starting pitcher (John Maine) had all gone on the DL than to any
cosmic realignment caused by our shifting our presence to France.
She might have a point.

Tomorrow marks only the 4th time in all of history that the
Baseball All-Star Game and Bastille Day have fallen on the same day.
The others were in 1953, 1970 and 1992. To me the only thing *less*
interesting than *that* fact is the All-Star Game itself.

I have zero interest in the game. I'd rather watch a regular season
game between the two worst teams in the majors than the All-Star Game.
At least in the regular season game the players are trying to win. Nobody
really cares about who wins the All-Star Game – not the players, not
the managers or coaches, and certainly not major league baseball. I've
already cited the evidence of this – the 2002 All-Star Game:

That game, as you'll recall, ended in a 7–7 tie. A *tie*?!? In baseball?!?

In the last several decades, in hockey and in pro and college football, the organizing bodies of those sports have gone to a lot of trouble enacting new rules as a way of eliminating ties in their games. Ties, they realized are detrimental to any sport. It is "the thrill of victory; the agony of defeat" – right? There is no mention of the "ambiguous emotions of the tie." I mean the point of a game is to determine a winner and a loser. The point is not to determine who is a "tier." And, oh how the hockey and football people envied baseball where there was no possibility of a tie.

Some times in spring training "games" there might be a tie, and that is understandable. Because the point of a spring training "game" is to get the players in shape and hone their skills for the games that you do want to win – the regular season games.

So in the 2002 All-Star Game, after 11 innings and the score tied, the Commissioner of Baseball, Bud Selig, who was probably only at the game because he was from Milwaukee and he thought he'd stop by and see his mum, decided that the fans had seen enough baseball for one evening and so he said, "Good game! Both teams played well. Let's call it a tie and go get a beer." If the Commissioner of Baseball doesn't care if there's a winner of the All-Star Game, then why should I?

t.

15 July 2009 – Gilbert, AZ. 85234

Terry,

We had an All Star Game yesterday. I watched. The President of the USA threw out the first pitch. Do I care that he, as a sportswriter said in the paper, "throws like a girl"? No. Or that he bounced the ball ... couldn't get it up to the plate? Don't care. But I would say this. None of the heads of the Latino nations to our south, nor the head of Japan, I suspect, would throw like a girl or bounce it up there.

S.

16 July – Lyon.

Steve.

I didn't see the All-Star Game, for reasons I covered in my last. But after your skewering of the President of the United States in yesterday's e-mail – a President I voted for and whole-heartedly support – I searched the internet to see if I could find a tape of the ceremony.

You're totally right; it was embarrassing. And here I thought we'd elected a young, athletic President; didn't they always make a big deal of his daily one-on-one basketball games during the campaign? Instead, we have a guy who clearly would be the last guy picked in any schoolyard pick-up baseball game in the country.

t.

(ps- Do you think our feminist readers will object to your phrase "throw like a girl?")

22 July 2009 – Gilbert, Arizona

Dear Terry,

I hope you had a nice anniversary celebration. I remember your wedding well. It was fun being your best man, and your and Miranda's guests were very supportive of me when they laughed at my rambling toast. The next day, at a gathering at your place, I sang "Old Shep" for your mother, always her favorite song of mine.

Now you are in France imagining that returning to New York will help the Yankees. Earlier this year you wrote, "They should move Jeter over to third and call me up for short. Rodriguez is due back in 30 days and I know my body would hold up for that long."

I know it would, too. It isn't as much about the body in baseball as it is about skills and practice.

I agree with you that the All-Star Game has no "meaning" if a game of ball can ever have meaning. Yet I sure enjoyed watching it this year. And for some reason, the honor of playing in the game stays with a player, even after death.

As in this passage: "Ray Boone, an American League All-Star infielder who was the patriarch of the first three-generation family of major leaguers, died Sunday at a hospital in San Diego. Boone, who lived in Rancho Santa Fe, California was 81."

That was a newspaper item from a few years ago that I'd clipped because Ray Boone was one of our heroes growing up in Detroit and following the Tigers as we did. He was a third-baseman who rolled his sleeves up a bit when batting, which back then was stylish and unorthodox.

Boone was an All-Star in 1954 and 1956 with the Tigers and was the American League's co-leader for runs batted in, with 116, in 1955.

But he was mostly remembered as the father of Bob Boone, who caught for 19 seasons in the majors and later managed the Kansas City Royals and the Cincinnati Reds, and the grandfather of the major league infielders Bret Boone and Aaron Boone.

Three generations of major league Boones. There are two other three-generation baseball families: Gus Bell, his son Buddy and his grandsons David and Mike, and Sam Hairston, his son Jerry and his grandson Jerry Jr. But the Boones were the only three-generation baseball family in which every member was an All-Star.

Because of the studies done in the three books I told you I read … the ones that challenged the issue of athletic "talent" and revealed the hidden power of practice, I believe what happens in families like this is that these kids all practice more, play more, than other kids do. And are sent to the best baseball camps and programs.

Practice is a major reason I love watching baseball. Ray Boone was not smoothly quick or athletic or "blessed" with any kind of body.

What's the opposite of practice?

How about a player I'm following who got a big contract, millions of dollars, his own local TV show, opened a restaurant, took long, long marlin-fishing trips with celebs, etc. and was no longer able to hit a curve, a slider or a change-up? And, being unable to hit those three pitches, which he gets a steady diet of now (because he can't hit them), pitchers can fire a fastball past him now and watch him swing late and tangle himself up in the batter's box like a twister. He's out of practice. He let himself go. His timing is gone.

Here's another thing about baseball that's strange. The effect it has on politicians! I read an interview with a woman who is a nationally known politician, I won't say who she is, but she's a person recently nominated to one of the highest positions in the land, and they asked her if she liked baseball and she said no, she didn't really have time to follow it. Now, that answer is fine with me! Somebody asks me about hockey or NASCAR and I'm going to give the same answer and I don't expect them to hate me for it.

But here's where it gets strange. A few weeks later I see the same woman on TV and she is now saying, in answer to another reporter's question, that yes she is a real baseball fan. Really? The reporter asked her what team she followed most closely and she said, "The Senators."

Of course, there is no such team.

When you and I were boys there were Washington Senators until 1960 when they moved to Minnesota and became the Twins. Then later, for ten years, from 1961 to 1971 there was a reborn Washington Senators team until it moved to Texas and became the Rangers.

Right now there are Washington Nationals, the worst team in baseball, which we here in Arizona are grateful for, so we ourselves don't have that distinction.

I see by your itinerary on my wall that you have about two more weeks left in France, then back to NYC. Kathy and I are looking forward to seeing you there in August!

Steve

23.vii.09 – Lyon, France

S.

If you had told me before today that Mark Buehrle was making $14 million a year, I would have suggested that it seemed a mite high. I'm pretty sure I never made $14 million in my life ... so far – though the royalties from these classic books push me closer each year.

To be fair to Mark, I've never pitched a perfect game either. As he just did today. Which prompted me to seriously look up his record. I'd, of course, always been vaguely aware of him; after all he's been a starting pitcher in the American League for 10 years now. But I was surprised to see that he's won 133 games already, and he just turned 30.

I'd be surprised if anyone ever wins 300 again in our lifetime the way they coddle pitchers these days, but it seems to me that Mark, who's a control pitcher and doesn't seem to get hurt ... well, he might have a shot.

Jamie Moyer is the closest active player to 300 (among those who haven't already made it) at 255, but the guy will be 47 at the end of this year and it'll take him at least three more good seasons to get to the 3C mark ... I don't think so. Halladay, maybe. Especially if he signs with the Yankees who'll give him plenty of run support, but he's at least 9–10 years away too.

Anyway, after our earlier no-hitter discussions, it's good to see a couple already this year.

What's more rare than a perfect game? How about an unassisted triple play – there've only been 14 in the last 109 years of major league history.

I'm sure you remember the Oriole shortstop Ron Hansen. He owns one of the 14. He did it on July 30, 1968. The previous one was more than 41 years before that, on May 31, 1927, by Johnny Neun of the Detroit Tigers. Think of that: more than four decades without an unassisted triple play.

You know when the one before Neun's was?

The day before – May 30, 1927.

I'm especially fond of unassisted triple plays, because I once made one.

It was in an advertising agency softball game when I was in Canada. I was with Grey Advertising at the time and we were playing our client Lipton.

Runners on first and second, no one out, and I was playing short. A line drive over second that I was able to get to and then stepped on second for two outs. The runner on first was halfway down the line to second when he saw what was happening, turned around and started back to first. I could have easily thrown the ball to first to complete the triple play.

But though no one else understood what was at stake in terms of personal glory, I did. I was pretty sure that I could beat the runner back to first running and I took off after him, tagging him out two or three steps from first. Unassisted triple play!

Yes, I know it was a glory-hound play. I should have just thrown to first, but then, of course, it wouldn't have been unassisted. And if I'd have been a manager I would have torn a strip off me, but it was just a slow-pitch, advertising agency game and I'd never made an unassisted triple play ...

25 July:

Obviously I wrote the above several days ago, but I've been afraid to send it for fear it might jinx the Yankees' winning streak.

Since the All-Star break, the Yankees have been fantastic; they've won 8 in a row. Over the same period, Boston has gone 2–5. So right now we're in first place by 2½ games. I *knew* my coming to Lyon would change their fortunes!

Another thing that I'm sure has helped the team quite a bit, I think, has been my *personal* involvement with some of the games. In Lyon, unlike Paris, I've got internet access in the apartment; therefore, when the Yanks play a day game (as 3 of the games on this winning streak have been), I can actually follow it, pitch by pitch, on mlb.com.

Day games in New York start at 7pm here and while Miranda sometimes insists on going out to a restaurant to dinner instead of watching a computer screen with me for a few hours in the early evening, we are usually back here in time for me to catch the last few innings. While I "watch" the game, Miranda is reading *War and Peace* on her Kindle. So I really don't get why she rolls her eyes every time I boot up the Yankee game; I mean, she's just glued to an electronic screen too, right?

Night games in New York start at 1am here, and don't end until 4 or 4:30 so I skip those. Though, I suppose if it were a *really* important game I'd have to sacrifice some sleep. Anyway, as you can see, I'm basically rational about all this and that's why I realized it was ridiculous thinking that writing you during the win streak would "jinx" anything.

However, if the Yankees lose this afternoon, well, don't bother looking for any correspondence from me during a win-streak for the rest of the season.

terry.

Patagonia, Arizona - 25 July 2009

ter.

Kathy and I packed our bags for a weekend in Patagonia, Arizona, a charming little village a few miles from Nogales, where rain and relaxation were promised to us. Rain is hugely positive and romantic to Arizonans.

In Patagonia, we stay in her brother Bill's silver Airstream trailer, great for rain on the roof. Same kind of trailer that Lucy and Desi had in their classic movie *The Long Long Trailer*. In fact, this trailer is done up nicely with some portraits of Lucy and Desi inside, and lots of retro 50s decor.

I took my big, thick, wonderfully entertaining copy of Joe Torre's *The Yankee Years* with me to read. I've been reading this book a little at a time since we started this baseball correspondence. It's a moveable feast, this book. And you know that Torre now manages the Dodgers who lead our division. And it's just too much fun to read about all the intellectual mistakes the GM Cashman made over the years trying to catch up to what he perceived to be the Red Sox superior sabremetric statistical research. Heartbreaking! To read about how Bernie Williams was let go against Torre's wishes and replaced by two losers whose stats looked good but whose character was bad and who ended up not being able to be reliable pinch hitters and back-up guys for the Yanks.

So Kathy and I are heading down the highway from Phoenix to Patagonia talking about how the Diamondbacks themselves tend to get rid of good players and replace them with bad ones when a couple miles up ahead a horrendous traffic accident occurred. I quickly told Kathy that in Jean Luc Godard's movie *Weekend* the world ends this way! In a massive traffic jam. She hadn't seen the film.

It turned out that a fifty-year-old woman was at the wheel of a huge tractor-trailer truck when she veered off the road and lost control of the vehicle. It exploded into flames, toxic at that. She was killed instantly. Her husband, who was sleeping at the time in a back compartment of the truck, survived and is okay. Now in stable condition. He was sound asleep when the big truck rolled over and blew up. Redefining, forever, for him, the phrase "rude awakening."

Traffic was stalled for four hours!

But we finally made it to Patagonia and went to a little restaurant called The Home Plate. It had baseball pictures on the wall, mostly of the Cubs from years gone by. There was a photo of the restaurant's owner shoveling snow from his Chicago home driveway with the caption, "This is why we are HERE!"

Oddly, on the wall, was a big oil print of Baseball Joe! The fictional book character from the 1930s, and the hero of the antique book I sent you at the start of the season, *Baseball Joe at Yale*.

The next morning we went back there for breakfast. Kathy snapped a picture of me next to Baseball Joe to send you. Kathy then had what she described as the worst scrambled eggs in her entire life, while I had a marvelous omelet they called "The Kitchen Sink" which had so many delicious ingredients I couldn't finish it.

I read the Tucson paper over breakfast and caught up on their home baseball team The Tucson Toros. A former Diamondback, a former All-Star, Junior Spivey, is attempting a comeback with the AAA Toros. Kind of a sad story but the eggs were good. At least to me. Seemed like that omelet had everything but the kitchen sink thrown into it.

Patagonia is a favorite hangout of the wonderful novelist and poet Jim Harrison, who has a home here. He says he hunts quail and loves the area. I haven't seen him here, but I now remember that you met Harrison in Paris once, *n'est ce pas?*

Jim Harrison once wrote, "Naturally we would prefer seven epiphanies a day and an earth not so apparently devoid of angels."

Prefer that to what? Because I would say that we ... you and me ... have got that already.

S

July 30, 2009 – Lyon, France.

dear steve,

Lyon has been very good for the Yankees. Today we are in first place, 3½ games in front of the Red Sox. But more than that – take a moment to look at the standings: which team has the best record in the majors?

Trick question because two teams are tied for that honor. One is managed by the last Yankees' manager (the Dodgers under Joe Torre) and the other is managed by the current Yankee manager. I wish the season would end right now, but instead there are some 60 nail-biting games to go.

Still, I'm glad the Yankees are in good shape with a bit of breathing room because I'm afraid I wouldn't be able to suit up should Jeter go down. Well, I could suit up but they'd have to order a larger uniform. Despite not having missed a single day of my 3-mile fast walk while we've been in France, I've managed to put on 4 kilos since we've been here (that's 9 pounds to you). More power perhaps?

I feel yesterday was a watershed not only because the Yankees got to the best record in the majors, but also I turned 65. This event involved yet another huge kilo-packin' dinner.

Despite the usual negative associations of turning 65, I'm not in the least put out.

The way I see it, 65 is the new 64.

But now that I've got you here, let me tie up a few odds and ends I've been meaning to deal with:

The day before yesterday a new record was set for most games pitched in by a Jewish pitcher. The new record is 553 games and it was set by Scott Schoeneweis of your Diamondbacks. Of course, Scott sets a new record every time he pitches, which might not be very often now that his ERA is up to 7.13.

You cannot believe how much coverage Michael Jackson's death got over here. I mean no one was ghoulish enough to actually *go to his home*, but you couldn't pick up a paper or turn on a television without seeing his carefully sculpted face. The left-leaning newspaper *Liberation* had a 20-page section on his life; the whole paper is usually only 36 pages.

Was it that nuts back in the States?

By the way, Facebook offered me the chance to vote on whether I thought an official Michael Jackson national holiday should be created. Call me a stick-in-the-mud curmudgeon, but I voted against.

Being in the city of silk, everywhere we turn there is a bit of silk or silk-industry history or stories. I'd like to add my own small story:

A number of years ago when I was in advertising, I was working on the National Fur Council account and the industry was having a very big problem with PETA, People for the Ethical Treatment of Animals. The members of this organization would go around committing terrorist acts on people they felt were opposed to the ethical treatment of animals. Like women wearing fur. Various people in favor of ethical treatment for animals would attack these women on the streets and spray-paint their fur coats. Some women are sensitive to this kind of attack and the fur industry was worried that it would put them off buying fur coats in the first place.

We were asked to look at this problem and see what could be done. Well the first step was to do a bit of research on PETA. One of the women I was working with knew someone who was in the organization and we arranged an informal meeting over drinks at a nearby bar. This guy was very nice and he was quite open with us about PETA and what it stood for. He had even brought ads they were running some of which showed the faces of very cute-looking rabbits and baby otters while the headlines suggested they were about to be shipped off to the gas chambers.

When we told him that most of the fur used in coats was made from animals raised on farms specifically for their fur, he explained that PETA's objection to fur wasn't a question of ecology or preservation of the species. It was, instead, exactly what the name of the organization suggested; they were for the "ethical" treatment of animals and they considered killing animals "unethical." But they also objected to wool because the sheep get very nicked up in the shearing.

I was wearing a wool sports coat at the time and started feeling guilty. Thank God my pants and shirt were cotton. But then he told me that my leather shoes and belt were also offenses. And finally ... my tie!

"Is that a silk tie?" he asked.

He told me PETA was very opposed to silk. Apparently silk worms spin cocoons and then the silk manufacturers put the cocoons in boiling water until the worms are dead. This is because if the worms were allowed to come out of the cocoon, they would break the strand of silk that forms the cocoon and then be useless in the making of my Yale Club tie.

I told him not many people are aware of PETA's stand on silk and that they really should be running ads showing the faces of very cute and sympathetic-looking worms.

Which leads me to another animal issue. It seems you have a new dog – a love-at-first-sight puppy judging from the pictures you sent. Congratulations. I would, however, ask that you please not mention this dog when you come to New York in August.

If news of the dog does somehow get out, I'd like you and Kathy to go on endlessly about how much trouble a dog is ... how he ties you down so your life is no longer your own ... and generally make out that it was the worse decision you've ever made.

You see Miranda is dying to get a dog. We can't get a cat because she's very much allergic to them. But given our life of constant travel, a dog would be a disaster. To be fair, she only brings up this desire about once a week, usually after having seen someone's cute puppy in Washington Square Park or in the elevator in our building. She gets really out of hand, however, after our stay on Georgian Bay each Fall when for five or six weeks we're given the loan of an absolutely lovable schnauzer named Samson. On my better days I like to think of myself as the number one male in Miranda's life, but it's clear that each Fall I slip into the number two spot behind the admirable Samson.

Anyway, after very narrowly managing to avoid acquiring a dog all these years, I can imagine the pressure I'd be under if she found out *you* had one. ("Well, Steve and Kathy have a dog and they travel a lot. They say he's no trouble at all.") So mum's the word.

By the way, how'd you come up with the name Jimmy for your dog?

My grandfather Hill was given a dog when he was in his early 60s. As you know he was a real baseball fan and when it came time to name the dog, he said we'll name him after whoever gets the most hits for the Tigers in this afternoon's game. Apparently the pitcher they were facing that day had his stuff going and he pitched a 2-hitter against the Tabby Cats (as desperate sports writers used to sometimes call the Tigers). Both hits were by the same player – second baseman Jerry Priddy.

So Jerry became the dog's name. I just looked up Priddy (the human) and discovered he was not a bad ballplayer. 11 years in the majors, most of them as a starting second baseman. And it would have been 13 years if it hadn't been for the two he missed because of World War II. He must have been a hell of an athlete because I remember that after he retired from baseball he became a professional golfer.

I think I've only ever been to one PGA golf tournament in my life. It was at Oakland Hills in Birmingham. Anyway I can't even remember what the tournament was but I do remember that Jerry Priddy was in it. He wasn't a big star on the tour, but I followed him for several holes. Just because he was a former Tiger, I suppose. And, I guess, because my grandfather's dog was named after him.

I could even picture a scene in which I introduced myself to him between holes and told him about Jerry – the dog. Well, I could picture how *my* role in the scene would play out, but I couldn't quite picture his. So the scene never took place. Too bad, in retrospect I'd like to have seen his reaction.

t.

Gilbert Arizona – 1 August 2009

Terry,

I hear you about Miranda wanting a dog. And I can see why you don't want one, given all the travel you do. It really would be unworkable. So, now what? Here is, I believe, your best option: *Be the dog.*

You, yourself, become the very dog she wants. Because otherwise you'll have to get a dog. Be mindful that when a woman "wants a dog" it's because, as you fear, she has run out of patience with you. She's heard all your best material, seen your best moves when you were younger. So she now "wants a dog."

You have to *be* that dog, Terry. At first, it will feel new to you. But picture this: She comes home and you're on the living room floor, on all fours. Looking up at her lovingly. (And because of the skater generation you can get awesome kneepads these days.) Don't overdo it, but little things here and there. In a romantic, intimate moment where you used to say something sweet and gentle, this time you bark. Things like that.

And yes I will tell Miranda about nothing but the nightmarish aspects of owning a dog. I won't tell her that he's enriched our lives and brought joy into our world. I'll leave that out when talking about Jim.

How did we name Jim? (I love your grandfather's story of Jerry the dog.) Our vet asked us that same question a month ago and I said we named him after James Joyce, and the vet raised his eyebrows and started talking about *Ulysses* and Molly Bloom, which surprised me as I was only joking, trying to cover up the fact that he was named after James T. Kirk of *Star Trek*. A movie we had just seen.

We had kicked around way too many names for him. In fact, he had a name already when we got him as a puppy. His name was Latte. We couldn't handle that name. My daughter Mar, who manages a coffee house, gave him that name. It was cute, but too cute for a manly little Jack Russell blend with a fantastic vertical leap. So we searched for names and I thought of the star ship Enterprise, and thought of Scotty,

Spock and Mr. Sulu and those were also too cute. I wasn't telling Kathy that I was mentally doing this but from the kitchen I suddenly said to her, because I was totally inspired, "Jim." The captain of the starship!

She then said, "Jimmy!" And the dog looked up at her and began wagging his tail. "Jimmy!" she said again and again. And so it was.

S.

7 August 2009 – Back in New York! USA.

steve,

Several months ago I said I wanted to write you about my favorite baseball books. This was prompted by having read the book you gave me before the season started – *Baseball Joe at Yale*.

It was really quite an interesting book … it was also terrible.

You said that you'd read it some 50 years earlier when you got it from the Birmingham Library. Well, I would say that 10 or 11 is probably the right age to read that book if there *is* any right age. 64 was definitely the wrong age.

To be fair to the author – Lester Chadwick – the book was not written for 60 year olds. *Baseball Joe at Yale* and all thirteen other of the "Baseball Joe" books, which were written between the years 1912 and 1928, were aimed at younger readers. The series starts when Joe is playing sandlot baseball and is probably about the age of most of the readers of these books. Through the series Joe goes from predictable triumph to predictable triumph in sandlot ball, high school, college, the minor leagues and the majors. By the end, Joe is a team owner.

The plots, which always include an obvious villain who Joe eventually defeats, are pretty pedestrian. But it's the writing itself which makes one cringe – no baseball cliché is spared. Why, for instance, would a writer ever call a pitcher a "pitcher" when alternatives like "twirler" or "fireballer" are available? And why write "home run" when "4-ply clout" or "quadruple bagger" say the same thing so much more colorfully? It was really quite funny to read.

I was curious about the author Chadwick and so I looked him up. It turns out that his real name was Howard R. Garis and, as one article claims, he may have been the single most influential writer of fiction for the young of the 20th century. He was a prolific writer who wrote under half a dozen pseudonyms. In addition to the "Baseball Joe" books, he also wrote the "Uncle Wiggily," the "Tom Swift" and the "Bobbsey Twins" books among others.

There have been two biographies written about Garis, one in 1966 and a second in 2007. Both are written by descendants so I wonder if either mentions what some of the articles do, which is Garis's patent anti-Semitism. I never saw any evidence of it in *Baseball Joe at Yale*, but apparently in some of the later books in the series, the villain is a conniving Jew who is frequently just referred to as "the Jew."

But enough about a bad baseball book; below is a list of my ten favorites. They are listed in no particular order because these books were read over a period of 40+ years and it would be folly for me to be making the fine distinctions needed to decide which of two books should stand at eighth or ninth on the list when the books in question might have been read 35 years apart. So:

- *Bang the Drum Slowly* (Mark Harris)
- *The Southpaw* (Mark Harris)
- *It Looked Like Forever* (Mark Harris)
- *The Universal Baseball Association, J. Henry Waugh, Proprietor* (Robert Coover)
- *Don't Let Baseball Die* (Art Hill)
- *The Long Season* (Jim Brosnan)
- *Ball Four* (Jim Bouton)
- *The Baseball Abstract* – 1982 (Bill James)
- *Moe Berg: Athlete, Scholar, Spy* (Kauffman, Fitzgerald, Sewell)
- *The Celebrant* (Eric Rolfe Greenberg)

You'll note that Ring Lardner's *You Know Me Al* isn't on the list. It was a book I very much liked but it just didn't quite make the ten.

As a tribute to Lardner's book, however, you'll find three Mark Harris books on the list. I honestly believe that Harris picked up the format for his Arthur Wiggins baseball books directly from *You Know Me Al*. All four of the novels are in the first person and told by a semi-unschooled ballplayer.

You may question why some baseball books you have loved aren't on this list, *Money Ball* for instance. The reason is simple – I haven't read them.

Interestingly exactly half of the books are novels while the other five are non-fiction. And maybe that non-fiction percentage should be even higher because you'll see only Bill James 1982 *Baseball Abstract* is listed while, in fact, I've read and learned from a number of these Abstracts. But the 1982 edition was the first I read and had the most influence on my baseball thinking and I thought it would kind of defeat the purpose to list other years' editions.

Finally, as I warned you several months ago, one of the books on the list (*Don't Let Baseball Die*) was actually edited by you. It was also written by my father. But, why, you may ask, didn't I include his second book *I Don't Care if I Never Come Back*. Didn't I like it? Well, yes, I did. I liked it a great deal, but I thought it was essentially the same book (albeit in different words) that you and he originally cooked up two years before.

Enough! How about your list?

t.

8 August 2009 – Gilbert, Arizona

Dear Terry,

Wow I hadn't realized *Baseball Joe* was a bad book, having loved it 50 years ago (how time flies when you're having fun) and I'm amazed that you still read it! Thank you for your academic devotion to this project.

My favorite baseball books are:

- *Money Ball* by Michael Lewis
- *The Summer Game* by Roger Angell
- *Ball Four* by Jim Bouton
- *Men at Work* by George Will
- *Coach* by Michael Lewis
- *How Life Imitates the World Series* by Tom Boswell
- *Doc Ellis in the Country of Baseball* by Donald Hall
- *The Baseball Abstract* by Bill James
- *The Yankee Years* by Joe Torre
- *Northanger Abbey* by Jane Austen

I put the Torre book on there because it was the one I was reading this year.

I put Michael Lewis number one because I believe that *Money Ball* is the best baseball book ever written, just as I now consider *Blind Side* by the same Michael Lewis to be the best football book ever written. A close second in the baseball category is *Coach* by Michael Lewis. Lewis has also written the best books on Wall Street I've ever read, and is now one of my five favorite living authors, up there with Tom Wolfe, Peter Abrahams, George Dawes Green and Terrence N. Hill.

Now our readers have some new books to read! This is the book that keeps on giving, no?

Oh okay, I knew you'd notice it.

Northanger Abbey by Jane Austen?

No I haven't actually read it. But British author Julian Norridge uses Jane's book to help prove his assertion that baseball actually originated in Britain! His book is called *Can We Have Our Balls Back?* He refers to Jane's book because when introducing her tomboy heroine Catherine Morland, Jane writes, "It was not very wonderful that Catherine, who had nothing heroic about her, should prefer cricket, baseball, riding on horseback, and riding around the country at the age of 14, to books."

That was written in 1798, long before the Abner Doubleday myth of baseball starting up in America.

But who cares? As far as I'm concerned, baseball started in 1955 when you and I started throwing to each other.

And now we're talking *baseball* in Arizona! Our Diamondbacks are fired up and hitting the baseball, running the bases and winning games left and right and it is exciting to see.

The guy I could not stand to watch (he was a starter hitting .195 through August 5) has finally been benched and our new manager Hinch is making daring moves and even got himself THROWN OUT of a game for arguing last night. Passion has arrived to this city.

Too late, of course, to make the playoffs. But it's fun to watch. Even guys who used to let us down in the clutch are putting wood on the ball and moving runners around! It's contagious!

I love watching this sport. And now, finally, I even love watching this team. They are playing as if their lives depended on it! I think all people love watching that, in the arts and in sports. Total, masterful, daring self-expression!

As you know I make my living coaching people in businesses. When people make the journey from failure to success it's because they finally agree to go through a two-step process: 1) Play your business as if it were a game. 2) Play the game as if your life depended on it.

The end of the season in any sport is most fun to watch because of this "as if your life depended on it" factor. We wait all year for the basketball playoffs, because who wants to watch regular season games with millionaires dogging it all night long? Same with baseball. It gets fun when the box scores now have a WILD CARD RACE box that gets bigger and bigger as the end draws near.

Terry, I'm glad you're back in America.

This is where you want to be. And, yes, your Yankees are in a hot, hot race to the finish with the Red Sox once again. And even though the D-Backs are not in the same situation, they *are* fired up and can't wait to be spoilers! It's that time of year.

Steve

9 August 2009 – New York, NY

Steve,

When we flew back from Paris to Newark the day before yesterday, we got back to the apartment here in New York at about 2 in the afternoon. From there, we made it our goal to stay up until 9pm before going to bed. If we went to bed immediately, we'd never get our bodies back on a North American clock. But boy was it tempting to take about a four or five hour nap the moment we got to our place because we got up in Paris at 5am yesterday morning to make our flight. This means we'd been up since 11pm *the night before* by New York time.

The trick to keeping awake, of course, is to stay very busy. So we unpacked. I did my 3-mile exercise walk (which I hadn't had time to do in France before we left). We went shopping at the supermarket. I sent off the piece on baseball books to you. Then we started digging into our piled-up, two-months' worth of back mail.

But even after that, it was still only about 6 – three eyelid-drooping hours to go. Now Miranda ordered Chinese food and we watched the Six O'clock News.

At 7, the Yankees-Red Sox game came on. We kept one eye on the game and another on the clock. Finally it was 9 and we could go to bed. At the time the Yanks and the Sox were wrapped up in a tight pitchers' battle with the titanium-necklace-enhanced AJ Burnett dueling the Red Sox' ace Josh Beckett. I watched through the sixth and the score was 0–0 when I went to bed.

I woke up at 5 this morning (I'm not totally on NY time yet) and went to the computer to discover that the Yankees won a great one on a two-run homer by A-Rod in the 15th!

We're now in first by 4½ over the Red Sox and own the best record in the majors. Now that we're in New York again I'm feeling very confident about my ability to maintain this lead for the Yankees.

A couple of things about our baseball books lists:

1) I totally forgot George Will's *Men at Work*. You're right; it was a terrific book and should have been in my top ten.

And 2) I think it's interesting that in my Ten, there were 5 non-fiction books and 5 novels. Your Ten was *all* non-fiction except for *Northanger Abbey*, which you acknowledged you haven't read. I suppose this means that you're more grounded in the real world while I'm a dreamy story-seeker. Probably true.

See you and Kath in a couple of weeks.

t.

10 August 2009 – Gilbert, AZ.

Terry,

This is what I say to the sportswriter in this morning's Arizona newspaper: What *are* you ... a 12 year old child?

Because he has a big story about how the "bright spot" in yesterday's D-Back defeat in the nation's capitol to the worst team in baseball, Washington, is that Mark Reynolds hit a home run. And that ties him with Pujols.

I don't like home runs. Not like I used to. Not like when I was 12 and home runs were the bomb. Remember Rocky Colavito? He didn't win many games for teams, but oh those home runs. Charlie Paw Paw Maxwell? Remember that he used to hit home runs on Sundays? Like clockwork! How exciting.

For a child.

But today, all grown up, I like singles. They keep rallies going. They force a pitcher to get frustrated and pitch from a stretch. They move things along. They don't require that the pitcher make a "mistake" by misplacing a pitch in the "wheelhouse" of a guy who swings from the heels but rarely helps his team win.

We have just been swept by the worst team in baseball. Swinging from our heels! But nothing was arriving in our wheelhouse! Pathetic.

Things are exciting elsewhere in the west however. The Dodgers are the best team out here, and it's so nice seeing manager Joe Torre succeed. Also: the San Francisco Giants have my favorite player in baseball, the player they call Kung Fu Panda! He is so much fun, and he has no wheelhouse! He hits everything! Balls, strikes, wild pitches even, he will swat them for a base hit! And he's jolly and full figured. He laughs a lot during a game. A roly-poly man like Donovan sang about.

Donovan prophesied the coming of Pablo E. Sandoval! *Here come the roly-poly man, and he's singing songs of love.* Sandoval has transformed the Giant dugout. After years of having a bitter, edgy dugout, irritated daily by Barry Bonds' insect-eyed 'roid rage, it's fun now to be a Giant. And they are good!

S.

14 August 2009 – New York, NY

Steve,

Have you noticed that every time one of us makes a comment on how well our team is doing, they start doing badly?

I talked about the Yankees' superb post-All-Star Game record on July 30th and starting that *very* day they lose three straight to the White Sox. On August 8th, you mention the Diamondbacks getting hot and next thing you know, they get swept ... by, as you point out, the *worst* team in baseball.

All of which is why I refrained from writing you much while the Yankees were finally carving some flesh off the Boston Red Sox in a great series (Aug 6, 7, 8, 9) which we swept 4–0. Interestingly, there've been four Boston-Yankee series this year and each one has been a sweep. Boston taking the first three and the Yankees this last.

We're sitting 6½ in front of Boston right now and I'm feeling very good.

Coming back from the gym the other day I passed a bookstore with a rack of remaindered $1 and $2 books out front. What caught my eye was a banged-up copy of Donovan's autobiography. This after you'd just mentioned him in your last e-mail. ("There are no coincidences." *sdc*) It would have been interestingly self-deprecating if he'd called the book *The Roly-Poly Man*, but instead it's called *The Hurdy Gurdy Man*.

I almost bought the book for you before it suddenly struck me how short life was and what percentage of it you'd be willing to devote to reading Donovan's life story.

But the roly-poly man is Pablo Sandoval. Well, you see that's the problem with baseball today. There are no longer 16 teams with 25 players each for a total of just 400 players to keep track of. Now there 750 players to keep track of so when you mention how much you like Sandoval, I'm thinking I don't even know this guy. I mean I've seen his name up there with the league leaders in batting average but I couldn't begin to picture him.

Fortunately the Giants are in town this weekend so I bought tickets to go to Sunday's game at the new Mets Stadium. I'll check him out. But I am already intrigued; the guy's 5'11" and weighs 250! He just turned 23 a week ago – could be the next Kirby Puckett. (Kirby was listed at 5'8" 210.)

The Mets themselves are long gone. They're 10 games back in the *Wild Card* race. They do have an excuse that even I give credence however. Three of their top four offensive stars are basically out for the season. Jose Reyes, Carlos Delgado and Carlos Beltran. Plus their number 2 starter – John Maine.

Tough luck. But New York is not a town with a lot of patience, and following two successive September collapses in 2007 and 2008, this season is not wearing well with the fans. I suspect there'll be some big changes in the off-season.

Anyway, I've got to sign off because I want to watch a baseball movie on television tonight – *For the Love of the Game*. Ever seen it? A terrific film. Kevin Costner made three baseball movies and I guess if you *made* me announce my favorite, I'd have to say *Bull Durham* because everybody loves it and you're crazy if you don't, right? But the truth is I'd be very tempted to vote for *For the Love of the Game* if no one was looking.

So what's your favorite baseball movie?   t.

15 August 2009 – Gilbert, Arizona, 85234

Terry.

I, too, love Costner's *For the Love of the Game.* I love the scene where his girlfriend says to him, "What if my face was all scraped off and I was totally disfigured and had no arms and legs and I was completely paralyzed. Would you still love me?"

And he replies, "No. But we could still be friends."

And thanks for not buying me the Donovan book, but thanks for the thought, too. I saw him once in Berlin and it was ethereal and wonderful. Back in his heyday. I still think he wrote some memorable tunes.

I hope you enjoy watching Roly-Poly Sandoval. He's an even better bad pitch hitter than Vladimir Guerrero. (Funny how many

Cubans were named after Russians like Lenin. I read last week that they've run out of toilet paper in Cuba, so the economic system they once embraced is not as exciting to them as it once was. Memo to Cuba: Out in the woods – if you'll remember our youth in Michigan – you can use leaves ... in a pinch ... but really truly do be careful about poison oak and poison ivy.)

Cubans are a great people, however, and it shows up in their music and on the ball field.

Actually I'm sure it shows up elsewhere, too, but where else am I looking?

In my seminars and training sessions I used to have the hardest time teaching the value of coming from nothing. Of being neutral. Of not carrying the baggage of the past into a conversation. It always sounded too Eastern. Too Zen. Then came Costner and his *Love of the Game* baseball movie. In it his character, a pitcher, resurrects his career on the mound by learning to "clear the mechanism" before throwing a pitch. Emptying his mind. When I talk about it that way and cite the movie, people in the workshop start smiling and nodding their heads.

Love to Miranda ...

S.

17.viii.09 – NYC, NY

steve,

Yesterday, Miranda and I went to see the Mets in a day game. We hadn't been to the new stadium all year and now, with the Mets basically out of any chance for the playoffs, it really wasn't all that hard to get tickets.

For less than a third of the cost of the Yankee seats we'll be sitting in a couple of weeks from now, we got basically the same seats we'll have for that game. Though obviously we were in Queens rather than the Bronx. Miranda is partial to the Mets and so perhaps her opinion that the Mets' Citi Field is being better than the new Yankee Stadium should be discounted.

But I agree. Or maybe it's just more to my taste; Citi's built on the retro model like the Baltimore stadium and Comerica Park in Detroit. It's a fun place to watch a ball game.

It's also a park that encourages pitchers' battles. It's a long-ball graveyard. And as happy as the pitchers are about that, I'll bet David Wright's privately wishing they'd shrunk the stadium just a bit.

In the last four years, Wright's averaged 29 homers and 112 RBIs a year. This year he'll be lucky to wind up with 11 and 65. Is he just having a bad year at the plate? No, in fact he's hitting .324, just a point behind his career best .325.

Wright's power was a moot point in this game, however, because the day before yesterday the Giants' pitcher Matt Cain beaned him and put him on the 15-day disabled list. So now all four of their pre-season All-Star players – Delgado, Reyes, Beltran *and* Wright – are on the DL.

The game was great though, you would have loved it. Mike Pelfry for the Mets and Jonathan Sanchez for the San Francisco Giants were both stingy in giving out hits and we went into the bottom of the ninth with the score tied 2–2. Jeff Francoeur started the Mets off with an infield single; they then bunted him to second and then Daniel Murphy lined a single that allowed Francoeur to score from second – a very satisfying walk-off win.

Then last night I watched the Yankees lose badly to the Mariners on the Left Coast. The only thing that cheered me in their 10–3 loss was that the Mariners' hitting genius Ichiro got 2 hits and is now only 25 away from his 9th straight 200-hit season in a row.

Put that in perspective: Tony Gwynn with a lifetime .338 and over 3000 hits had a high of 3 200-hit seasons in a row. Wade Boggs (.328

and also over 3000 hits), never managed more than 2 in succession and 7 overall. Pete Rose hit 200 hits in 10 seasons – but never more than 3 times in a row. Hell, *Ty Cobb* could only do it 3 times in a row.

But how about *this* statistic: Ichiro has currently gone more than a full season – 160+ games – without being held hitless two games in a row! The man's unbelievable.

t.

19 August 2009 – Gilbert, Arizona

Ter,

I love Ichiro, too. He just keeps smacking those singles, no matter who's on the mound.

In fact, I gave myself his name this year.

My business coach Steve Hardison had just done a marvelous job of getting me to see that in a recession, with corporations not having so many big expensive conventions, I should shift my own business tactics.

Instead of going for the fences with big paydays for keynote addresses and seminars at conventions that don't exist right now, why not shift to smaller contracts with small businesses and individuals? He said to me, "Home runs are great, but singles win ball games."

So I began a series of smaller contracts and had my best month in a year! Each day when I woke up I looked at the top of my Commitment Page under the category of Created Future and saw the code word ICHIRO. I am ICHIRO!

I don't need to be Babe Ruth.

This is yet another example of how all aspects of personal and professional life get better when you introduce a little baseball.

See you in NYC!

S

August 31, 2009 – Gilbert, Arizona

Terry,

What a trip that was! Thank you and thanks to Miranda for producing and directing such a fun-filled, baseball-packed week for us.

Of course I'm on a controlled two day fast right now to restore my body and longevity. We ate such wonderful meals with you!

(In the 1930s a study was performed on earthworms that demonstrated the extension of life due to fasting. The isolated worm on a cycle of fasting and feeding [my current cycle] outlasted its relatives by 19 generations, while still maintaining its youthful physiological traits. "The life-span extension of these worms was the equivalent of keeping a man alive for 600 to 700 years" the scientists said.)

I wouldn't want to live *that* long, but the principle seems good, no?

Here are my notes from the trip that I entered into my daily journal each night before going to bed:

Sunday, August 23: We arrive in New York. We love the hotel Terry and Miranda recommended to us, the brand new Hampton Inn. It has a huge balcony and wide panoramic view of the NYC skyline, and to the left we see the Hudson River! Wow. And waiting for us in the hotel room is a whole packet from Terry, full of maps, magazines, and articles, including a great article on Ichiro!

Monday: Off to the MOMA with Terry's passes, thanks for leaving them. I wanted to see the Cezannes, especially because one of my coffee cups has a Cezanne still life on it that I see every third morning, so beautiful. Great to see the originals, although I must say the colors look better on porcelain! Don't quote me on that ... then later that day to the Staten Island Ferry where we sail past the Statue of Liberty and the New Jersey shoreline to Staten Island to see the S.I. Yankees play the Oneonta Tigers. Fun games played by 20 and 21 year old boys, just out of high school and college, old enough to be our grandchildren! But big and strong and farm-fed ballplayers.

Tuesday: We are off by car to Saratoga today ... beautiful car trip through lush, green, winding, hilly topography of New York State, so alien to those of us who live in the desert of Phoenix, and so beautiful. We visit the Horse Racing Hall of Fame. Fascinating!

Wednesday: Up early to see the morning workouts at Saratoga. Beautiful track! Then back to the hotel to pack our bags for tonight's ride to Cooperstown, then back to the races. We see Rod Stewart at the races. Then we realize it's a look-alike.

Thursday: We are at our bed and breakfast in Cooperstown, New York, today, having arrived late last night. What a cozy place and what a charming town Cooperstown is. Today we went to the Baseball Hall of Fame and saw the plaques of all the elected players. I especially liked the Babe Ruth exhibit, with a short film and absolutely great black and white photo display. Terry and I were photographed by the Hall plaque of Al Kaline, a favorite player of ours when we were growing up in Detroit together.

Friday: Terry and I got our gloves out of our suitcases and played catch out on the grass in front of the courthouse yard in Cooperstown today. Baseball scouts driving by slowed their vehicles down when they saw how we moved, like naturals; then when they saw I had silver hair and Terry had no hair they sped their vehicles up shaking their heads. I know what they were thinking, *How come the people who really know how to play this game are all over 50?* Then a nice long scenic drive back from Cooperstown into Manhattan. Later in the evening Kathy and I go to a wonderful performance of *Our Town*. In the play a very poignant scene has the young hero quit the baseball team to get married and start an adult life. Insane sadness.

Saturday: It's off to Yankee Stadium, the new Yankee Stadium. Wow. It's really an amazing stadium, full of comfort and a huge jumbo-tron screen for replays and entertaining shots of the players and fans throughout the game. Yankees won 10–0. Yankees look like the best team in baseball. Derek Jeter was marvelous in the field and at the plate. The subway ride to and from the game was fun. Off to bed, totally worn out.

S

1 Sept 2009 – Williamstown, Massachusetts

steve,

We're back on the road after a brief two days in New York, this time on our own. Driving from the city up to our friends' beautiful place on Georgian Bay, Canada, where we usually go in the fall. I did, however, manage to pick up your e-mail in Hudson, New York, where we spent last night in a motel that pretty much resembled a crime scene.

What surprised me in the telling of your visit was that you did not mention what was one of the highlight incidents for me. It was while we were at the Staten Island vs. Oneonta game.

Our seats were in the front row on the first base side, about even with the coaching box. Before the start of the game, Miranda bought a huge box of popcorn which we were passing around among ourselves when an Oneonta coach who'd been watching infield practice wandered over and said hi to us. I offered him some popcorn, which was probably the reason he came over in the first place, and he stood and talked to us for a few minutes.

He was a former major leaguer, originally from Puerto Rico, named Luis Quinones. For the last three years, he's been the first base and hitting coach for Oneonta.

He jokingly chided Miranda for not getting butter on the popcorn and then asked us where we were from. I asked him if it wasn't a bit strange for him, coming from Puerto Rico, to be living in a small town in the middle of New York State. He said he liked it, that the place was nice and that he genuinely liked the people.

He was an open, friendly guy with an easy way of striking up acquaintances. This ability has no doubt served him well over the years. During an 18-year professional playing career, Luis played for 5 different major league teams and, by my count, 14 minor league teams, several of them more than once. This is a guy who's constantly meeting new people.

He was in the majors for 8 seasons and, though his lifetime batting average was only .226, he was a member of the 1990 World Champion Cincinnati Reds. Pete Rose was once his manager. And on the glorious day of September 3, 1989, Luis was named National League Player of the Week. I doubt there are many people in the world that remember that, but I'll bet you a buck to a grand *he* does. The guy will never get a single Hall of Fame vote and I'm sure you could buy his rookie card for a nickel and get a few pennies in change, but for more than thirty years, Luis Quinones has made a living, playing or coaching the greatest game there is. I would have traded a lot for that.

It was fun talking to him and he came over a couple more times between innings during the game, probably looking for some more popcorn. At one point I asked him which of his players he thought we might see in the majors some day. He said he thought the first baseman might make it and the third baseman. Of the third baseman he said, "He was a high draft choice and he hit for some power in college … so, yeah, maybe. Though he's not hitting at all right now."

"Who's his hitting coach?" I asked with a straight face. Quinones laughed.

[Just for the record, Steve, the first baseman's name was Rawley Bishop and he finished the season at .282. The non-hitting third baseman was Wade Gaynor who wound up with a .192 average. On the face of it, neither would seem to have an express ticket to the majors, but you never know. While looking up their averages on the internet, I also checked the Oneonta team from four years back, and right there on the roster was an outfielder named Clete Thomas. This would be the very same Clete Thomas who I saw hit a grand slam home run to help the Tigers beat the Angels earlier this year. You never know.]

I took my three-mile-exercise walk today in the town of Kinderhook. It's a picturesque New York town and a pleasant place to walk. At one point I passed a baseball field and saw a dozen kids, maybe 11- or 12-years old, playing a pick-up game. The pitcher for one of the teams was a girl – and from my brief glimpse of the game, it looked like she could really bring it. The game goes on.

I might add that we were in Kinderhook, as you've no doubt already guessed, to visit the ancestral home of Martin Van Buren – Lindenwald. I've never been to Elvis's home, Graceland, but I imagine the scene is pretty much the same. I mean the place was swarming with Van Buren groupies in a general frenzy, and people were constantly shouting out "Ol' Kinderhook Lives!" and "James K. Polk was mediocre!"

Still, it is one of those places that one simply has to see during your life. Miss you guys on the trip.

terry

Sept. 2 – Gilbert AZ

Terry,

Bingo! The one place in the world Kathy and I have been that you and Miranda have not! Graceland! (Kathy's actually been twice.)

I went a few years ago because I had business in Memphis. I had a speech to give at a hotel that was famous for little ducks walking through the lobby at some precise hour every day.

And I have to say that Graceland was a letdown. It's small. Especially compared to how we thought of it when the legend was alive. It was like Camelot in our minds.

Human imagination is amazing, isn't it? Blake said, "Imagination is the real and eternal world of which this vegetable universe is but a faint shadow."

But expectations diminish reality. That's my quote on this subject. Same was true of Cooperstown's Hall of Fame. All my youth I imagined it like the Taj Mahal. And it's just a building. Like a spruced-up American Legion building. But my expectations for the town itself and the car trip were non-existent, and voila! they were huge fun.

Our boyhood fantasy baseball games were huge and exciting. And as great as baseball itself was, it was never as glorious as it was in the mind.

This vegetable universe loses again! I've always loved William Blake. When we were growing up in Detroit and had to read his poem that had the line, "Tiger, tiger burning bright" I would think of Kaline in his hot, hot rookie season.

    s.

3 September 2009 – On the road in St. Catharine's, Ontario, Canada

Steve,

Just time to drop a quick note before we drive to Toronto. I used to have a client who ran his business on a simple formula which he revealed to me as:

$$H = R \div E$$

Happiness is Reality divided by Expectations. This is the positive spin on your "expectations diminish reality." My client ran a large supermarket chain and he cited this formula as the reason he would often have unadvertised "in store" specials. Customers would come in the store expecting only the usual and suddenly, quite by surprise, they'd come upon Triscuits at half price! Well, you can imagine the happiness.

Anyway, I'll bet the Taj Majal is dinky.

I'd also bet that you meant to say Kaline's hot, hot *sophomore* season when he was Blake's Tyger. His rookie year was quite passable at .276, but his second season he won the American League batting crown; it was then we suspected we had a future Hall-of-Famer at Briggs Stadium.

Miranda and I had dinner with my long-time friend, and one-time minor league team owner, Terry O'Malley and his wife at a restaurant here in St. Catharine's last night. (You met him once at a ball field in Toronto and it was only about 35 years ago so you should remember him quite clearly.) Anyway, he's a serious Yankee fan and so I'm reasonably certain we bored Miranda and Barbara to death talking about the season so far.

I'd told him the title of the book we were working on and he reminded me of one of the hoariest of baseball clichés. Whenever a ballplayer hits a little fluke dribbler or a wounded-duck pop fly that manages to drop in for a cheap single, some grizzled baseball man will say: "It'll look like a line drive in the box score tomorrow."

It will.

t.

4 Sept. 2009 – Gilbert AZ

Terry,

Many English Poetry anthologies have it as Tiger instead of Tyger for the very same reason that Chaucer's original stuff and even Robert Burns' work was given a bit of a chance. Burns otherwise is

> Thou need na start awa sae hasty,
> Wi' bickering brattle!
> I wad be laith to rin an' chase thee
> Wi' murd'ring pattle!

Not the kind of thing you want to stand up on a table and recite in a biker bar.

But I know what a poetic stickler you are! And I also know you have disciplined yourself to be a profound autodidact in the field of poetry, home-schooling yourself for years and years (I even once found a few years ago a copy of "The Waste Land" open in your bathroom) and journaling the ongoing tab of all the poems you have read.

More important was the correction of the Kaline season. We all forget his freshman year, don't we (all but you), given his sophomore brilliance.

It occurs to me now that box scores are a kind of poetry. Compact, yet loaded with symbols and inscape.

Steve

ps- If we ever write a book about football, we might call it *Two Guys Read the Defense.*

7 September 2009 – Gilbert, AZ 85234

Dear Terry,

Still resting up from our vacation with you in New York. It was so great watching Derek Jeter in person that afternoon jump up for that high drive – on its way into the outfield, he knocked it down, picked it up and got the man forced at second. What an amazing athlete, not only in his skills but in his total full-out efforts … how he runs out everything full tilt, how he plays with such energy and intensity.

If we could all do our jobs that way! What a world it would be.

Not like back home here. Where the morning headline describing the D-Back loss to Colorado was "Beyond Simply Terrible." And here's the opposite of Jeter: young Justin Upton, full of talent, an all-star, who on many occasions I have noted to Kathy while we watch the games *does not run unless he thinks he has to.*

Yesterday he hit a long, long deep fly to center that looked like it might, just might be a home run. But rather than run, Upton stayed near home watching, admiring his long hit. But lo! An ill wind swirled in the outfield (it's Denver!) and blew it back to the wall and onto the field of play! Omigod, thought Upton, I better hightail it to first! And rather than get the double or triple that a hustler would have gotten, he barely beat the throw to first!

He was taken out of the game.

Great move by the manager Hinch. But after the game Upton said, "It's one of those things that happens and you learn from it." Really? It was one of those things that just happens? Almost by itself? I hate the era of no responsibility in sports.

Like Rick Pitino. The Louisville basketball coach who got a waitress pregnant. In the very restaurant the night she served him! He said he made a bad choice. He said sometimes in life you make bad decisions. He was married and coach to young athletes and had sex with her in the restaurant anyway, a bad choice, like picking the wrong horse at the track? Then he paid her thousands of dollars for an abortion. He later said he didn't know it was exactly for an abortion. It was for something medical, he knew that. Heck, he just wanted her to be healthy! I can't wait till he plays Duke this year. And Kentucky. Those fans are tough with explanations like that.

I shouldn't be so depressed about the D-Backs, though. So what if their games now are beyond simply terrible. I noticed that when we all were riding the Staten Island Ferry back from the farm game in Staten Island, looking out over the night lights and rippling water, you pointed out that Spalding Gray jumped off the very same ferry to take his life. I'm not that depressed. It's just baseball. Right?

S

11 Sept 2009 – Georgian Bay, Canada

steve,

Have you noticed that the regular season is over? Technically, of course, that's not true; the Yankees, for instance, still have 21 games to play. But the fact is we already pretty much know who's going to be in the playoffs in both the American and National Leagues.

This seems strange; usually there are some hot races going with a lot on the line at this time of year. But look:

The Yankees, Angels and Tigers are all coasting to playoff spots by winning their divisions; likewise the Phils and Cardinals in the NL. The only real race is in the NL-West where the Dodgers currently hold a 2-game lead over the surprising Rockies. But it doesn't really matter who wins because whoever it is, the other team looks a cinch to get to the playoffs as the NL wildcard.

The only thing resembling a race in the American League is the Red Sox versus the Texas Rangers for the AL wildcard. I'll give you 3–1 and take the Red Sox if you're interested in losing some money to me.

Now here's the thing I love about baseball: even though the teams are already decided for the playoffs and it would seem that we should all just set our alarm clocks for October 7th when post-season play begins, I'm still totally fascinated. There are still so many storylines to play out.

Like … Derek Jeter, who will probably tonight get his 2,722nd hit as a Yankee. This would give him one more than Lou Gehrig's total and give Derek the most hits of any Yankee in history.

Like … how about Brad Ligue, last year's spectacular closer for the Phillies. The guy was perfect with 41 saves in 41 opportunities. This year he can't get anyone out. He's got a 6.97! ERA and he's already blown 10 opportunities. He won't blow any more this year though, because the manager just announced that he isn't their closer anymore. How can a guy go from being so great one year to so awful the next?

Like … the return of Pedro Martinez. The Mets gave up on him before the season started and didn't sign him. Pedro rehabbed in the

Dominican Republic and bided his time. When he was ready he cut a deal with the Phillies. There was a lot of skepticism. I mean the guy's 37 years old, often injured and a bit of a flake. He's been with the team a month now and he's 4–0. The way he's going, he's likely to see some action in the playoffs.

Or like ... Ichiro! Now only 5 hits away from his ninth 200 hit season.

Like ... will there be a 20-game winner this year? Starting pitchers only have 5 more starts in the season. That means only a handful of pitchers even have a mathematical chance at winning 20. My prediction is that only one will make it – Adam Wainwright, who's got 18 right now.

Like ... the Arizona Diamondbacks. At the start of the season your hopes were so high, but this morning their Elimination number is 1. Any D-back loss or Dodger win and they'll be eliminated for 2009. If they lose too many more, I think they'll be eliminated for 2010 too.

The point is, even though for all intents and purposes, the regular season is over I still check the scores and pour over the box scores with great anticipation each day to see how the hundreds of side-storylines play out. It's a great game.

And then ...

The Playoffs! and the World Series!

t.

12 September 2009 – Gilbert, Arizona

Terry,

Many say they "pore" over the box scores, but you say you "pour over the box scores" reminding me of a song I liked by the group Bread. The song was called "If." The lyric you reminded me of:

> And when my love for life is running dry,
> You come and pour yourself on me.

But I truly agree with you. No matter how "my team" is doing it's impossible for my love of baseball to run dry. So many fascinating aspects. Not like me watching the Arizona Cardinal football game this Sunday and when the game was clearly a lost cause I throw up my hands and curse and cuss at the TV screen and walk out of the room. The game is essentially over.

Baseball is different than that. There's always still something to watch.

However, when I look at the Diamondbacks' box scores these days I'd like to pour something over them. Coffee. India ink. But the rest of baseball is still, as always, fascinating.

You know something? When you and I were in Cooperstown throwing the ball back and forth, I noticed something. *Holding* a baseball is fascinating in and of itself. Just holding one prior to throwing it to your friend. And I found a quote from Roger Angell that I liked. He said, "Any baseball is beautiful. No other small package comes as close to the ideal design and utility. It is a perfect object for a man's hand. Pick it up and it instantly suggests its purpose; it is meant to be thrown a considerable distance – thrown hard and with precision."

That was us on that lawn in Cooperstown. Throwing hard and with precision.

S

19 Sept 2009 – Georgian Bay, Ontario, Canada.

steve.

I was going to write you yesterday to once again point out how great Ichiro is.

Last Sunday, as I'm sure you noted, he reached 200 hits, making him the only player in history to go over 200 for nine seasons in a row. The record of eight straight seasons had stood for over a century. Fittingly, the record was held by an Ichiro-like hit-meister, "Wee

Willie" Keeler whose motto, you'll recall, was "Hit 'em where they ain't." I'm sure Ichiro's motto is similar, though probably in Japanese.

Then the night before last he got a walk and two hits in seven plate appearances. His last hit, predictably a single, won the game for the Mariners in the 14th inning. What I was going to point out was that despite his walk-off heroics and two hits, his average went *down*. Coming into the game he was hitting .354 and after .353.

Then last night he got his second walk-off hit in two nights when he hit a 2-run *homer* in the bottom of the ninth to give the Mariners a 3–2 victory over the best team in baseball – the Yankees. And against the best closer in baseball – Mariano Rivera who had been successful in 36 consecutive save opportunities.

Oh yeah, and this time Ichiro guarded against his average going down by getting 4 hits in the game. His average is now .357!

terry.

26 September 2009 – Gilbert, Arizona

TNH:

I second your emotion on Ichiro. Did you know that Ichiro is his FIRST name? His last name is Suzuki, but when he broke into baseball in Japan there were four Suzukis on his team so he convinced the owners to let him put ICHIRO on his uniform and go by that name, just like Elvis needs no last name. Nor does Jesus for that matter.

They said from the start that he used his bat like a samurai sword ... and that he could cut a flying mosquito in half with the precision of his sword-swing. I also know that he is more disciplined than other players. He works harder, and even does a SQUAT, a deep catcher's squat ritual before every game, (similar to the one I taught you on the trip) which is why he has never had back problems.

The reason I taught you that squat was because I don't want you to have back problems any more, and I eliminated all of mine forever by the method taught by my friend Matt Furey, (he's a collegiate wrestling and international martial artist champion.) It's very simple. You go into a catcher's position. While squatted down you can even make some pretend throws back to the pitcher. You can do a visualization if you like. I did that. I pictured Frank House, Red Wilson, Johnny Bench, Lance Parrish and all my other favorite catchers. That keeps you down there a while, which is the point. Stay in the catcher's position as long as you can. Then get up. Repeat this process at least THREE times a day. And you'll never have a back problem again.

Tomorrow we are going to the baseball game at Chase Field in downtown Phoenix. The last home game of the year for the lowly Diamondbacks. I can't wait for the playoffs. When the real fun begins. But tomorrow will be fun, too. Just because it's baseball.

S

Sept 28, 2009 – Yankee Town!

Steve,

The Yankees clinched the division championship last evening, winning 4–2 against the hated Bosox. And while that was the big news, the game also marked two other statistical milestones:

It was the Yankees 100th win of the season. A feat no other team in either league will accomplish this year. This from a team that started the season unimpressively at 16–17.

The win also meant that we tied the season series with the Red Sox. After losing the first 8(!) games against the Beantowners, the Yanks won 9 of the last 10 and finished the Boston series at 9–9.

All in all, a glorious season. Which will all be forgotten in a heartbeat if we don't get to the World Series.

The game itself was a typical Yankee win this season. Solid pitching by Pettitte, who started; a "turn out the lights" save by Mariano; a homer by Teixeira; timely hitting by Matsui.

Now I know that everybody talks about how the Yankees buy pennants with their deep, deep pockets and there's no denying the contributions of Sabathia, Burnett, Teixeira and, don't forget, Swisher – all off-season acquisitions.

But the heart of the team is Jeter, Posada, Pettitte and Rivera. All four of those players were developed in the Yankees farm system and all four of them were on the team when they won the World Series back in 1996 – 14 seasons ago!

Now that's a little bit of a cheat because Posada was barely on the team that year, but do you know who the starting catcher on that '96 team was? Joe Girardi – our current manager.

Teixeira's home run yesterday gave him 38 and it seems likely he'll wind up leading the league in homers and RBIs, making him a leading candidate for AL Most Valuable Player honors. The other player they talk about is the Minnesota Twins' catcher Joe Mauer, who looks like he'll win the batting average title despite Ichiro's spectacular season.

But I'd like to put in a vote for Derek Jeter. For what I admit is the flimsiest of reasons – "intangibles." He can't parade the gaudy offensive numbers of Teixeira or Mauer, but he *is* hitting .333 and has scored over a hundred runs and he'll steal over 30 bases this year.

But there's also the leadership and the constant hustle and effort plus just plain smart baseball. I know this sounds strange coming from me, because usually I dismiss what the faux sports pundits call "intangibles" as being hopelessly sentimental and emotional.

Well maybe I *am* being sentimental and emotional about Derek, but let me leave you with one example:

Remember the play you commented on from the game we saw at Yankee Stadium? The one in which Jeter leaped in the air to knock down a line drive that had the word "double" written on it and then picked up the ball and flipped to second for the force out?

A great play, we both agreed. But later I checked that play on the play-by-play recap on the internet. You know how that play is written up in CBS Sportsline official play-by-play:

"Jayson Nix grounded into fielder's choice to shortstop."

Sounds pretty routine doesn't it? Not really the kind of thing they give out MVP awards for. And yet we *saw* the play and it was a heck of a play. Jeter does these unheralded game-winning things all the time. For instance I don't think anyone in baseball is better at going back into deep foul territory to catch fouls. But it's not the kind of thing that gets mentioned very often – and it doesn't show up in statistics.

None of this is to take anything away from either Mauer or Teixeira, both of whom not only hit for a ton, but also have won Gold Gloves at their positions.

This is the kind of semi-technical baseball talk that is fascinating to us, but I suspect will bore many of our hard-won readers to death.

t.

September 28, 2009 – Gilbert, Arizona

Terry,

Kathy, Deb and I went to the last home game of the year yesterday, and it was glorious, despite the lousy season for this team.

Young Billy Buckner (not related to former big leaguer Bill Buckner) pitched a good game and the D-backs won, 7–4. All three games we went to this year were D-back victories, starting with opening day, then the game we saw with you and now this final game at home.

I almost wish now I had not followed the season on TV and in the box scores so closely, and just based my experience of this team on the three games I saw!

This game was filled with great moments on and off the field. Late in the game they sent some young women out on the field to throw tightly-packed D-back tee shirts into the crowd, and Kathy leaned out and caught one! A great grab that won her instant admiration from the people sitting around us. Then, after the game was over, Kathy and Deb tried to get Mark Grace's attention up in the broadcast booth. (We were in seats down behind home plate.) Grace finally spotted the two waving women and flashed them a big smile and gave them a thumbs up. Given how much those two women have loved Grace since his Chicago Cub days (when they both lived there), this was no small moment.

Attendance was down 16% this year for Arizona. They say it was the economy, but I think it was the team's inability to advance runners when they were in scoring position. Buckner, our young pitcher up from the minors in the last months of the season, had a better batting average than six of our regular starters. He got a solid RBI single in this game.

I watched Chris Young, the D-Back center fielder who many say is the worst starting player in all of baseball (no argument from me), as he flirted with a .208 batting average when he got a hit. But it sunk back to .207 before the game was over. Why do they start him?

Because they have invested millions and millions and millions of dollars in him (no exaggeration) and because this team is no longer a baseball team but rather a corporation that talks in terms of ROI (Return On Investment.) Given all they've paid him, they just can't sit him down and take a loss on that investment, they have to just keep playing him looking for that return. Corporate ego.

Therefore they've used the Diamondbacks as a minor league rehab team for Young this year. Most teams would send a guy hitting .207 down to the minors to rehab his skill set. At least until he got his average up to .208. But not this team. This team is known for parading their expensive mistakes in front of the major league fans each game hoping to get their ROI. Corporate thinking versus baseball thinking.

But Baseball is about tradition. In my book. Traditions we love like the Yankee pinstripes. Or the old English "D"s on the Detroit Tiger home uniforms and caps. This corporation brought in some "branding" experts two years ago and changed the team colors! And uniforms! Now we are Sedona Red and Sandstone. What would Dizzy Dean have said about those colors?

Now I hope I'm wrong about everything. The beauty of baseball is that every fan can be a vocal critic, and find joy in that. Not like in politics where if you criticize a politician's policy it's because you are part of the lunatic fringe. I hope Chris Young bounces back and blooms and shines next year! (Has it ever happened? Can you do the research for me? That a player who played a full year and hit .207 and then next season hit .280?... which I think an outfielder should hit.)

I hope I'm wrong about our manager Hinch. I do know he's extremely bright. And I liked a lot of his managerial decisions this year. And *Moneyball*'s Billy Beane thinks he's perfect. So I hope I'm wrong.

And I hope I'm wrong about Sedona Red and Sandstone. I hope the colors maybe remind the world of the painted desert around Sedona, and that they might just be perfect for our future World Series appearance.

With a team like this, you hope you're wrong about everything.

S

ps- We had dinner after the game at Cooperstown, Alice Cooper's restaurant a few blocks from the stadium, same place we went when you were here. Alice is a huge sports fan and he lives in Phoenix. I've always loved his music. Especially "School's Out." *School's out forever!* Reminds me of baseball season.

5 October 2009 – New York, NY

steve,

Yesterday was the last day of the season. And since I already announced a month ago that the season was basically over as far as which teams were going to be in the playoffs, this should have been a very dull final day. But baseball has a way of making you look stupid, because, in fact, it was a fascinating day.

(Knowing how much you hate the use of the second person, I suppose I should re-phrase that last sentence and say, "Baseball has a way of making *me* look stupid.")

In the first place, the Minnesota Twins came from 5 ½ games back on the morning of September 13th to tie the Tigers for first place with one game left in the season. So first place in the AL-Central was still on the line.

Also there was the story of superstar Alex Rodriguez. This is a numbers story, which to the non-baseball fan may not seem of much interest, but *you* know how much baseball – far more than any other sport – is a game of numbers addiction.

For 11 straight years, A-Rod has managed at least 30 home runs and 100 RBIs. This year, however, he was destined not to make those numbers. He missed the first 28 games of the season with an injury. Which meant that coming into the season finale he had only played 123 games with 28 homers and 93 RBIs. You simply don't get 2 homers and 7 RBIs in one game. And at the end of the fifth inning with only four innings in the season remaining he still needed 2 and 7.

It only took him one inning to get them.

In the sixth, A-Rod hit both a grand slam and a 3-run shot to give him exactly 30 homers and exactly 100 RBIs for the season. Of course in order to do that, he had to tie the all-time record for home runs in an inning *and* set a new American League record for RBIs in an inning. But he *did* it – amazing!

You correctly pointed out when you were in the city that for A-Rod's standing in baseball's pantheon of great players to really glow, he's gotta win a World Series ring or two. He's also gotta perform well in post season. He's never won a World Series and his post-season performance as a Yankee has been awful. But, as the final game of the season showed – this is his year!

The Yankees will open the playoffs by playing the Tigers *or* the Twins. As you know, both of those teams won their final games of the regular season yesterday so they remain tied at the end of 162 games and the division title will be settled by a one game playoff tomorrow.

We're flying to Mexico tomorrow and I go with mixed feelings. Yes, I'm looking forward to being there and eating guacamole and drinking Dos Equis; but I *hate* not being in New York when the Yankees are in the playoffs. It's a great atmosphere with everyone in the city – baseball fan or not – being totally aware of what's going on and the bars jammed with cheering fans during the games. Go Yanks!

Terry.

6 October 2009 – Gilbert, Arizona

Terry,

I'm glad A-Rod has been forgiven for taking steroids and for dating Madonna while still married.

Bernard Baruch, who lived into his mid nineties and was sharp and energetic right up to the end, said "One of the secrets of a long and fruitful life is to forgive everybody everything every night before you go to bed."

Which brings me to the Zen master of forgiveness, in my book, Joe Torre, who whenever anyone would ask him about Manny Ramirez's behavior for the Dodgers this year would say, "That's just Manny being Manny."

If he fails to run out a fly, or shows at the plate in baggy clothes, or takes some steroids, it doesn't matter, there is no judgment, because it's just Manny being Manny. How could Manny not be Manny?

But isn't that true of all of us? I know your saintly and brilliant wife, the lovely Miranda, has often had to inform people that your unorthodox (and always funny) humor meant no offense to anyone. So I'm recommending that Miranda practice saying, "That's just Terry being Terry."

It's not exactly a get-out-of-jail-free card, but it's close. And it spreads the usefulness of blanket forgiveness. Something I'm learning from Joe Torre.

Love to you both, S

10.10.09 – San Miguel de Allende, Guanajuato, México

Steve,

You should pay attention to me; I am a seer. In my last letter, I told you that this is A-Rod's year. It's in the cards or the stars or somewhere.

On Tuesday, the Yankees opening night of the playoffs. We were watching in Mexico City at our friends' apartment. In the first, Rodriguez flied out with Jeter in scoring position on second. Immediately graphics started appearing telling us that A-Rod was now 0 for his last 29 at bats with runners in scoring position in playoff games.

I mean I know they don't have anything else to talk about, but c'mon.

The next two times up, both times with Jeter on second, A-Rod drove him home. The monkey was off his back! And the game was won 7–2.

A-Rod, as who doesn't know, is dating Kate Hudson right now. (I mean Madonna is *so* yesterday, don't you think?) After each A-Rod RBI, the camera cut to Kate cheering in the stands. I mean I have no idea what she makes in films, but I think the Yankees should pay her $25-million a year (the same as A-Rod makes) to stay with the guy; she's worth it.

Then the second game in the series last night ... and what a game!! Please tell me you watched it.

If you did, you saw Kate. My kind of girl, sitting front row in a $10,000 seat, cheering her man on. Well, it worked in the 6th, when the Yankees were trailing 1–0 and A-Rod drove home (Guess who?) Derek Jeter from second to tie the score.

But by the ninth we were behind again 3–1 and hope was fading. But Teixeira got a single and then it was A-Rod. The man is a cinch for the Hall of Fame, but this clinched it – he hit a homer that half the country was watching to send the game into extra innings. Oh to be in the Stadium when he did that! Or even just in a bar full of Yankee fans in the Village! But I'll tell you, it wasn't half bad in our TV room in San Miguel – I mean if the floor weren't concrete we would have gone through it. But the game still wasn't won.

Miranda *hates* extra innings – too stressful. She likes the kind of game we saw at Yankee Stadium: 10 to 0. In that kind of game you can go survey the souvenir shops; go look for the sushi bar; check out which hot dog stand has the best condiments; etc.

When it's 3–3 and extra innings in the playoffs you can't do that stuff.

I would say Miranda saw approximately 50% of the pitches in the last two innings. On the others, she covered her eyes – it was just too tense. But she's a game girl; she hung in there through any number of unbelievably nail-biting pitches until Teixeira led off the bottom of the 11th with a line-drive that demanded its way into the stands for the game-winning home run. We lead the series now 2–0 and need only one more win to move on. I'm not counting chickens, but I have started construction to a little shrine to A-Rod; it's modest, but still, I think, a fitting tribute to the man who allowed us to win that game. I'm working on a little Kate Hudson figurine to go on the shrine.

　　　t.

October 11, 2009 – Gilbert, Arizona

Terry,

It's fun holding the remote control switching back between football and baseball, always staying longer on playoff baseball.

What you wrote about Jeter, I agree with. We had a near all-star here in Mark Reynolds who finished second to Pujols in home runs, and is a player who plays hard and is a captain type, like Jeter, except for one thing. He strikes out more than anyone in baseball.

Jeter is great because he works the count. Every pitch thrown to him is important to him. He is a nightmare to a pitcher. And he's all the things you said he was. He's an energetic presence on the field and in the dugout. He wins the award that *you* used to win when we played as teens: "Team Sparkplug."

I remember that Michael Jordan once said of him, "I love his work ethic. He has a great attitude. He has the qualities that separate superstars from everyday people."

That's what I love most about watching him. He will outwork everyone else on that field. He knows how (through practice!) to bring all of himself to the ball park each day. And for a hero, those qualities are the best, because we can all do them. There isn't anyone alive who can't wake up in the morning and decide to outwork the world.

That was the miracle of Leonard Cohen for me. Reading his interviews I learned that he spent more time on each song than any other songwriter. Often writing a hundred verses before fine-tuning the final three or four for a song. Spending years on some songs. Bringing everything he had to a single line of lyric.

The Derek Jeter of songwriters.

S.

12 Oct 2009 – San Miguel de Allende, Mexico

Steve.

Get out the broom! The Yankees just swept the Twins to advance to the American League Championship Series.

I didn't see Kate in the stands on television so maybe she didn't go to Minnesota for the game. But she must have been watching somewhere because the third game was very much like the first two:

In all three games the Yankees have had to come from behind.

In all three games Kate's man A-Rod has been a hitting star. (In the final game he hit a homer that tied the game in the seventh.)

In all three games we've received great pitching from our starter. Each gave up only 1 earned run in 6+ innings.

In all three games Jeter was instrumental in winning the game – *twice* with heady defensive plays.

All in all a great series for the Yankees who were actually out-hit by the Twins 29–23. However, we hit 6 home runs to *zero* by the Twins.

I would have loved to have been in New York for the series because when it's post-season in New York, everybody talks baseball. Two days before we flew down here, we were having some work done in the apartment in New York and the plasterer, Tony, saw me put on a Yankee cap and he asked how I thought they'd do in the play-offs.

We talked for five minutes or so about their chances and who had to perform well and so on, but he saved his special regard for Mariano Rivera.

"What's he got – over 500 saves?" he said. "The guy's got *one* pitch! He just says, 'Here it is again; hit it.' They never do."

Mario in the series? He pitched in all three games. Three and two-thirds innings; no runs; seven strikeouts.

Meanwhile, the best argument for not having a major league baseball team in Denver is not the thin air that forces them to keep game balls in a freezer so that they don't fly out of the field in the thin air. No, the best argument is that they had to postpone the Rockies-Phillies game on Saturday because of snow!

When the make-up was played on Sunday, the snow was gone,

but the temperature was 32! I don't know if you remember your science, but that's freezing.

    t.

15 October 2009 – El Fuerte, Sinaloa, Mexico.

Steve.

We're on a train/plane/bus tour of the remote area of Copper Canyon in Mexico and sitting here at our second stop in El Fuerte I realize that for much of this trip I probably won't have internet access to send you e-mails. So I'll keep my own little diary and send it on to you when we get back to San Miguel.

Fact is, in some of these towns in the Canyon it's an open question as to whether I'll even be able to see the games on television. It's possible that the entire AL Championship series between the Yankees and the Angels could be over by the time we get back.

    t.

16 October 2009 – Ceracahui, Chihuahua, Mexico

steve.

Ceracahui has a population of 1,300. It's deep in the Sierra Madre Occidental Mountains. We're in a quite beautiful and comfortable hotel here that has its own picturesque vineyard. The rooms, however, are without phones or televisions. We knew this in advance and it would have been just fine with me if our two-night stay here did not happen to coincide with the first two games of the AL Championship series.

When we got here this afternoon by train I was already resigned to not having any news of the games until we get to the much larger town of Creel in a few days. (Creel's population is 4,000.) But as the shuttle bus pulled up to our hotel, sharp-eyed Miranda notes a small sign near the entrance that says "SKY TV." A glimmer of hope! At the desk Miranda asks if they get satellite television here and, pointing to the television in the lobby, the receptionist answers "si" but then it's qualified by "algunas veces." Sometimes.

I call this woman the receptionist because she apparently is the hotel expert on the satellite reception. She explained that the hotel is located in a valley so the reception was problematic and seemingly at the whim of shifting winds, cloud cover and the positions of the planets. This all sounds like astrology to me so I don't hold out much hope.

And yet! When we return from a visit to the local mission and a brief walk around the town, there are four Mexican guests from El Fuerte sitting around the television in front of the bar watching a blurry, double-vision version of the game.

Good enough for me.

Miranda and I sit and watch the whole satisfying 9 innings – a 4–1 Yankee victory. Sabathia is sharp as the starter and Rivera cleans up in the 9th for the save. A great beginning to the series.

terry.

⊖

17 October 2009 – Ceracahui

s.

I don't mean to make too big a thing of this out-in-the-middle-of-nowhere thing, but this morning Miranda and I went out for a walk and had to share the road with wandering horses and cows. In light of this remoteness I suppose I should be grateful for even this double-vision glimpse of the Yankee-Angels game. And don't get me wrong, I am.

It's just that it's tough. For one thing, it's hard keeping all the players on the screen sorted out. At one point in last night's game, for instance, there was a little pop fly that looked like it was going to fall in between two fielders; but in the end, they *both* caught it! – what I had mistaken for the shortstop and the left fielder was actually just the left fielder seen double on the screen. I might add that, though I only had a couple of beers last night, I've got a killer headache this morning – eyestrain. Which doesn't mean I won't be doing it again tonight for another 9 innings in game 2.

terry.

18 October 2009 – Ceracahui

s.

Well, I was wrong. I didn't stare at the double-vision TV screen for 9 innings last night; I stared at it for 13 innings when the Yankees finally won it 4–3 with the help of a wild throw by the Angel second baseman.

But the real Yankee savior was, once again, A-Rod.

In the top of the 11th, the Angels got a run to take a 3–2 lead. It looked as though we were headed for a loss. But in the bottom of the 11th A-Rod led off with a home run to keep us alive.

At the beginning of the game, Miranda and a number of guys in our tour group were watching the game with me, but by the time the Yankees finally won it, it was only me and a little guy from the hotel kitchen giving each other high fives. It was ten pass eleven here, but ten after one in the morning in New York where the game finished in a cold rain.

(I love this about baseball; I am in this little town in the Sierra Madres and here's a serious Yankee fan to watch the game with me.)

t.

19 October 2009 – Creel, Chihuahua, Mexico

s.

Well, yesterday was a travel day for both the Yankees and us. The Pin-Stripers moved from friendly but cold and rainy New York to the hostile beautiful weather of the West Coast, and Miranda and I moved from tiny Ceracahui to the relative metropolis of Creel (pop. 4000).

There's even a television in our room here and last night I watched a bit of the Phillies-Dodgers game on it; the reception is perfect!

t.

⊗

20 Oct 2009 – Creel

s.

I don't know about you, but I still find it hard to think of the Angels as the *Los Angeles* Angels.

I do, however, love and admire the bald greed of the name change from Anaheim Angels. The Angel owners discovered, by looking at population figures for the area, that Los Angeles is a much bigger town than Anaheim. Ergo, they said, we could draw fans from a much larger population base if we change our name to *Los Angeles* Angels.

This thinking is, of course, necessarily accompanied by a firm belief that you *can* fool all of the people all of the time. Because for this ruse to work, you have to count on the fans *not noticing* that the team is still playing in Anaheim at the same ballpark they've always played at. I am only surprised they didn't change the name to the *New York* Angels; think of the market they could have drawn from then!

No matter what the name is, I don't like us playing in Anaheim. Especially after last night's game there. We lost on a walk-off double in the 11th. Girardi used 8 pitchers.

t.

⊗

October 21 – Creel

steve.

But then we come back with a laugher win. Thank goodness I didn't have to sweat a bit. The Yankees won 10–1. Sabathia sparkles and A-Rod hits another dinger. We lead the series 3–1 and we only have to play one more game in Anaheim.

Having been a professional sportswriter for a few years, you are of course familiar with the problem of what to call teams when you're writing about them. I mean in the account of any game, you might have occasion to mention the team name 20 or more times in the course of the story. And often you might need to name the team twice in a single sentence. Now no writer wants to use *any* word 20 times in a 500-word article, and using the same word twice in a sentence, well, it just feels downright unprofessional.

The solution, of course, is to use synonyms. But because there are no real synonyms for the official name of the team – "Detroit Tigers," say; the sportswriters use their imagination and create them. Thus when we were growing up in Detroit, I can remember the Tigers at various times being called: the Bengals, the Tabby Cats, the Tabbies, the Felines and many other even sillier names in an effort to avoid using "Tigers" over and over again in a story. I even remember one sports news broadcast in which the Tigers were referred to as the "Nine-Livers." (It's a good thing it was a broadcast rather than in print, because sitting on the page, it kind of looks as if the team was a freak of nature, like those people born with 6 toes or an extra kidney.)

Anyway, I'm running into this problem a bit here writing these letters and have mentally offered pardon to those sportswriters whose made-up nicknames I used to chuckle at. In this same spirit I hope you'll pardon my use of "Pin-Stripers" in my entry of two days ago.

t.

22 Oct 2009 – Toluca, Mexico

steve.

Got up this morning in Creel and took a longish bus trip to the Chihuahua Airport. From there we flew to Toluca. So we were traveling all day and we didn't get to our hotel here until past 11 at night.

The first thing I did in the room is turn on the television only to discover that the Yankees lost 6–7. No details are given, just the score. I won't find out what went wrong until I get to a computer some time tomorrow.

It doesn't really matter, I guess; the bottom line is that it's now a 3–2 series. Thank heaven we're going back to Yankee Stadium.

    t.

24 Oct 2009 – San Miguel de Allende, GTO, MX.

S.

We're back home and so are the Yankees. But the 6th game of the series is postponed until tomorrow because of freezing rain. What do you think, is the season too long?

    t.

25 October 2009 – San Miguel.

Steve.

The Yankees are going to the World Series! The Series they haven't won since 2000, and haven't been in since 2003.

Sentimentally, I guess, I was hoping for a Yankees-Dodgers Series, but I suppose it's more fitting that we face the current World Series Champion Phillies. And that's what'll happen in three days when it's game #1 – C.C. Sabathia against Cliff Lee.

Miranda and I watched tonight's clinching game, sweating through the whole thing at home. In the end it was a 5–2 win. Pettitte was great. Rivera was great. Johnny D came through in the clutch. And try as the Angels might they couldn't get A-Rod out – he was 2 for 2 and walked three times. Wednesday will mark the very first World Series game A-Rod has ever played in.

The Yankees are going to the World Series!

t.

Oct 26 2009 – Gilbert AZ

Terry

Wow what an account of fighting through the split screen images to see your games ... and walking the roads among the cows and horses ... a close-up on a split-fingered fastball on your Mexican TV would look like a kind of four-fingered palm drop grip! You'd try to throw it and get clobbered!

I threw my arm out yesterday. How long since you've said those words? How long since you've had a sports injury? We joke about our ages. I think about the next book in our series and I think of the title *Two Guys Read the Charts at the End of Their Beds* would be good.

Wouldn't it be fun to die together? Nabokov's new book *The Original of Laura* arrived and the subtitle is: *Dying Is Fun.*

I threw my arm out playing with a tennis ball in the back yard with Jim the dog, who plays this game like Luis Aparicio. But my arm is sore.

Love to Miranda,

S

Oct 29, 2009 – Gilbert, AZ

Dear Terry,

Remember when we were sitting around the table in Cooperstown at that charming little bed and breakfast we were staying at? And the other couple who were guests from Philadelphia and great Phillies fans, able to solve for us why the Phillies' uniforms all had the black initials **HK** on them? (It is for Harry Kalas, longtime announcer for the Phils who died this year.)

We talked baseball that morning, and afterward as you and I walked out into the sunshine I said to you, "Beware the Phillies." Because I knew that you were so counting on the Yankees going all the way, and I knew, because of my almost mystical abilities to prognosticate on baseball, that the Phillies were the only team who could match up with them.

And now it's down to the Phillies and Yankees! It starts tonight. Unless there's rain or snow. Why, by the way, are we actually surging into November with this World Series? With winter winds? Players blowing on their hands before each pitch? Where are the "boys of summer?" Remember when we were boys playing when it was too cold to play and the bat stinging our hands if we didn't connect just right? Sometimes even if we did!

If the Yankees are determined to be a regular postseason team, why didn't they build a roof on the new stadium? And now with corporate avarice out of control we see basketball, hockey, baseball and football all being played at once. All pro sports all the time. Omnipresent.

The playoffs were great fun to watch. The Angels have a guy whose name is so fascinating, Chone Figgins, that I couldn't get over it. Right out of Charles Dickens was Chone Figgins. He played poorly, but I'll never forget him. I looked him up and found that he was acquired by the Angels in a trade for a player with another amazing name: Kimera Bartee. If we were writing a novel about baseball we couldn't use these two names because they look overly invented! Life out-writes fiction once again!

Omnipresent.

Interesting word I used back there. Omnipresent. I know I get in trouble whenever I digress too much from the book subject at hand and introduce something from what you see as my "wacky" world of personal spiritual growth. And I know from our Jane Austen days that you claim not to have a spiritual gene in your body. But can I just put this one quote in the book? It's from my favorite spiritual/ religious writer Robert Godwin (*One Cosmos Under God*). And it does relate to baseball I promise. Anyway, Godwin is explaining how a word like "omnipresent" when applied to God is rather meaningless:

"If you simply say that 'God is omnipresent,' there's really no way for the ego to get its little mind around the word 'omnipresent,' which is both bigger than big and smaller than small – you know? *It's far, beyond the stars / it's near, beyond the moon?* (Professor Bobby Darin, *"Somewhere Beyond the Sea"*). It doesn't compute, because there's nothing in our rational or sensory experience to match it. It's just an empty concept, like 'infinity' or 'nothingness' or 'Cubs win the Series.'"

Give my love to Miranda,

S.

29.10.2009 – San Miguel de Allende, MX

Steve.

I like Godwin's comment on the Cubs. They really do seem a sad-sack franchise. Especially when you consider that the last time the Cubs were even *in* the World Series my father was at one of the games *wearing his Marine Corps uniform*, having just returned from World War II – 1945. And, of course, famously, they haven't won the Series since 1908.

For me the strange thing is that most of the time they don't actually seem like a lousy team, the way, for instance, the St. Louis Browns or the Washington Senators always did when we were growing up. I look at the Cubs each year and think that if a couple of things fall into place, they could be contenders. A Cub season never looks like a Tetris game though, and those things never quite fall into place. I'm tempted to think of it as just bad luck, but 101 straight years of bad luck seems a bit much don't you think?

Like one day Ernie Banks walked into a mirror shop and accidentally broke 15 mirrors?

But to hitchhike on Godwin's theme of an empty concept – an idea that when scrutinized just doesn't make sense – I'd like to nominate a couple of hoary baseball notions that I think are ready for tossing in the trash.

One is the belief that looking at a player's performance in RISP (Runs in Scoring Position) situations means anything at all. Baseball "experts," including a lot of guys who should know better, always hold this stat out as the true measure of a clutch player. A-Rod was endlessly dissed regarding his horrible performance in his recent playoff appearances. There was some statistic that he hadn't performed in his last 20-some RISP at bats or something like that. If you look at the record, you'll see that what's being talked about is a total of 11 games in the playoffs from '05, '06 and '07. Every player who's been in baseball any time at all has gone through an 11-game hitting slump. It's an acceptable statistical variation.

The other reason the concept of "Runners in Scoring Position" doesn't make sense when you're talking about A-Rod is that every time he comes to bat there's *always* at least one runner in scoring position – and that's the batter, who in the case of Rodriguez is just one swing away from driving himself in.

If you look at A-Rod's overall postseason stats, you'll see that his batting average is .295 and he's hit a home run once every 14.8 at-bats. Compare that with his lifetime regular season figures of .305 and 14.2. Not far off.

Oh, but the commentators say, compare him to a *real* clutch player like Derek Jeter. Okay, compare him: Jeter's lifetime batting average is .317; in postseason play his average is .311.

A second notion baseball commentators talk about is the idea that bad teams leave a lot of runners on the bases – LOBs. Even you have fallen prey to this cliché in some of your comments about your D-Backs in this correspondence.

Yes, it's very frustrating when your team leaves the bases loaded several times in a game and you lose 4–3. But, the teams that lead the league in runs scored (clearly the best measure of a team's offense) generally also lead the league in runners left on base.

The Yankees led the AL in runs scored *and* in men left on base. Your maligned D-Backs? 8th in the NL in runs – 9th in men LOB.

No need to tell me to fear the Phillies, Steve. I've always feared them. Even more after last night's first game of the World Series. The Phils handled the Yankees as if they weren't aware that we are an offensive juggernaut.

Miranda and I watched every out of the game at home in Spanish, which is fitting given that almost half the Yankee team counts the language of Cervantes (and Ricky Ricardo) as their mother tongue. But the results were not good … so tonight we're going out to dinner and I won't even look at the score until about the 6th or 7th inning – I'm pretty sure this strategy will change our luck.

t.

Nov 2 09 (Day of the Dead) – San Miguel de Allende, MX.

Steve.

Here in Mexico there is a new rule outlawing spitting on the futbol field (that would be "soccer field" to you.) This is due to the fear of spreading swine flu. If they had this rule in major league baseball, the Phillies' shortstop, Jimmy Rollins, would have to take up a new line of work. Perhaps he could free-lance for various fire departments helping extinguish 5-alarm blazes.

I watched with great pleasure these last three games of the World Series – all of which the Yankees won, giving us a 3–1 lead in the series. But I was struck by how much Rollins spits. If the camera is on him in the dugout for ten seconds, you can make a lot of money by betting he'll spit at least three times.

Yes, all baseball players spit. But, really, Rollins's ability must be the envy of the league. It's an amazing skill he's developed and I expect (or expectorate) it's one of the major reasons for his NL MVP Award of a couple of years ago.

Just to finish this subject: Why *do* baseball players spit?

Other thoughts on those three games:

Miranda and I did not see the opening pitch of any of those victories. In addition, we saw at least a part of each game in bars in town. The first game of the Series (the loss) we saw every out at home.

Now you know I am not a superstitious guy, but I think that a pretty clear formula for a Yankee win is indicated here.

As much as I hate it when our entries take on a "Did you see that?!" nature, did you see Johnny Damon's brilliant play in the last Yankee win?

With the score tied and two out in the top of the ninth, Johnny got a single to bring up Teixeira. The Phillies put on the Teixeira Shift moving all the infielders to the right side of the field.

On the first pitch Damon stole second cleanly and then, with "The Splendid Spitter" Jimmy Rollins standing right behind him with the ball, Damon took off for third. I thought he'd be out a mile at third as

Rollins started to throw ... but then *didn't* throw. Because as Johnny realized, no one was covering third! The third baseman was over on the other side of second as part of the Teixeira Shift. Damon stole two bases on one pitch! The first was on speed, the second on brains.

After Teixeira was hit by a pitch, A-Rod lined a double down the left field line to drive in Damon for what wound up being the winning run.

We watched last night's game in a sports bar right off the main square in town. There were 25 or 30 fans in the bar (happily most were cheering for "Los Yanquis"). The atmosphere was definitely festive, but not for the game, but because last night was the major celebration of the Day of the Dead.

There were mariachis, skeleton costumes, black mourning garb everywhere, celebration altars, parades and all-night partying. Of all the nationalities, I think only the Mexicans truly understand how much fun the departed can be.

In the midst of these games I get an e-mail from a friend in Toronto who's not a rabid baseball fan but has watched a bit of the World Series this year and he asked: So when did the 7th inning stretch turn into a military exercise?

Good question. I mean the technical answer is obvious: right after 9/11. Suddenly we started singing "God Bless America" during the 7th inning stretch before "Take Me Out to the Ballgame," and it seemed to make sense at the time. But why does it continue now, eight years later? And it's usually sung by the very best singer in the laundry platoon of whatever branch of the armed services happens to be in town that day.

I think we should sing a different patriotic song between each inning: "My Country 'Tis of Thee," "America the Beautiful," "The

Marine Corps Hymn," "I Like to Be in America" from *West Side Story*, "This Land is Your Land," etc.

The only exception would be after the 6th inning; there we must bow to tradition and sing "YMCA" when the grounds crew does their little line dance while tidying up the infield.

(When I think about it, I'm surprised the Anti Muslim Defamation League, the AARP, the ACLU, the Jewish Defense League and all the major feminist organizations have not united to sue for an injunction against the playing of this song at ballgames. Clearly "YMCA" is a song that is pro-Youth, pro-Male and pro-Christian.)

Adios, t.

Nov 3 2009 – Gilbert AZ

Dear Terry,

I think it's a stretch to call the *West Side Story* version of "America" patriotic. If you listen to the lyrics there is a lot of sarcasm and irony in there about America. It's sung from the point of view of Puerto Rican gang members. But maybe that would be okay.

In fact, why not have non-patriotic, internationally flavored songs for balance? Songs from different nations to honor how multicultural we have become in baseball. I have always loved the song "Sukiyaki" which is the only Japanese song to ever be a hit in the USA. Imagine how good Matsui and Ichiro would feel if we all sang that song ... say in the second inning? Then maybe "La Bamba" in the fourth, etc.

I love watching the World Series. The tension and the drama are palpable.

(Picture Jeter singing: "Yo no soy marinero, soy capitan!")

S.

5 November 2009 – Gilbert, Arizona

Terry,

G.K. Chesterton was asked what book would he most like to have with him on a desert island and he said, *Thomas's Guide to Practical Shipbuilding.*

The Yankees won the World Series last night. We watched parts of the game at the bar at the Ritz in Phoenix, (it was our anniversary and night out), parts at Morton's Steak House, and listened to part on the radio in the car and watched the final out on TV at home.

To say that the Yankees purchased a world championship team would be curiously wrong. Yes they spend more than anyone on players, and they have finally done quite well at that (because they used to spend badly on pitchers who were strangely bad on the mound) because Teixeira and Burnett and Sabathia helped get them there and helped them win BUT … but … who really won this for the Yankees? The players that were Yankees all along: Jeter, Rivera, Matsui and Pettitte. Real Yankees not recently purchased as free agents.

So that was great to see … although I wanted it to go seven games so we could watch the last game in its entirety and I love a close fight.

The Yankees built a strong ship this year, and don't tell me other teams don't try to do the same thing with their purchasing. Even the lowly Diamondbacks have players they have spent tens of millions of dollars on. Like Eric Byrnes and Chris Young. The only difference here is that they were bad decisions. Tens and tens of millions and millions on players who shouldn't even be in the major leagues. Bad buys. Uninformed impulse buys.

I want you and Miranda to be happy. So I was not at all unhappy to see the Yankees win because I knew it would make you happy. (Even though I'm a National League guy, and really wanted the Phillies to put up a proud fight.

And now the season's sadly over.

And my heart quickens at the thought of spring training.

s.

5 Nov 09 – San Miguel de Allende, Mexico.

Steve,

The Yankees win the World Series!

We too saw the victory in several locations. We'd committed to going to a movie with friends last night so we went into town and caught the first few innings of the game in a bar down the street from where the movie was. (Though I purposely did not watch the first pitch because I know that helps the Yankees win.) When we were finally off to the theater, the Yankees had a tenuous 2–1 lead, thanks to a Matsui home run.

After the film, there was talk of getting a drink somewhere. I said fine *if* we went to a place with the game on. We went to a place called Harry's, it's very popular with the gringo crowd and the bar was jammed. I cheered when I saw the score was now 7–3. But it was only the top of the 7th so I sweated through the final nine outs.

It was scary in the 7th when the Phillies had two on and Chase Utley up. Utley had looked pretty much like Babe Ruth in the Series to that point, but we managed to get him out.

Then with one out in the 8th, Girardi brought in Mariano Rivera to get the final five outs. After the fact you say, well of course, Mariano would mow 'em down. But I still managed to sweat each batter until finally, on the tenth pitch to Shane Victorino in the 9th, he got him to hit a ground ball to Cano who threw to Teixeira for the final out of the Series!

It was all very satisfying for a season that started inauspiciously seven months ago with a 10–5 loss to the Baltimore Orioles.

The Playoff and Series heroes here are a parade: Matsui, who drove in 6 runs in the clincher and was named World Series MVP; Jeter who hit .407 in the Series; A-Rod, whose Playoff record this year is 15 runs scored and 18 RBIs in 15 games along with a .365 average; Andy Pettitte, who was 4–0 in the Playoffs, including wins in the clinching game of each series; or Mariano whose Playoff ERA was 0.56. I do believe, however, that the parade marshal should be Kate Hudson.

It's a great team, maybe one of the best Yankee teams of all time.

And I love the fact that when Joe Girardi took the Yankee manager job two years ago, he said he wanted to wear number 27. Now that he just managed them to their 27th World Series Championship, I hope he wears number 28 next season.

I want to correct an error in my e-mail from three days ago. On Johnny Damon's brilliant double steal, I said the catcher threw to Jimmy Rollins, but of course with the Teixeira Shift on, it would have been the third baseman covering second. And it was. Pedro Feliz received the throw, and it was he who realized, when Damon took off for third, that there was nobody to throw the ball to because he himself was the third baseman and he was covering second.

terry.

Nov 10 2009 – San Miguel de Allende, Mexico

Steve.

This morning at the gym here in San Miguel, I saw a guy I hadn't seen since the spring when we were here before. He'd noticed me doing my baseball exercises back then and asked me about them. I was wearing a Yankee cap today and he came over and told me that he was afraid Jeter was going to be set as the Yankee shortstop for a while.

Yes, I said, but you gotta remember, he's getting on in years. He's over 35 now; someone may need to take over, so I'll continue my fielding regime. And I believe they still have my phone number.

Of course, I was a little disappointed that I wasn't called up at some point during the season. But I'll settle for the Yankee championship.

This is the beginning of the baseball awards period. With the regular season over and the World Series hardware back where it belongs in NYC, Major League Baseball sort of relives the season by gradually releasing the awards. Every couple of days a new award is announced. MVP, Manager of the Year, Rookie of the Year, the Cy Young Awards, etc.

Today was the American League Gold Glove awards for the best fielder at each position. Two players we've talked about quite a bit in this correspondence were on it – Derek and Ichiro. I don't have to tell you how happy I was that Derek was picked after an absence of two years. I mean not only does the guy hit .334, score 107 runs and steal 30 bases (at 35!) but he's also named the best fielder in the league at the toughest position.

And Ichiro. In every one of the nine years he's been in the league he's had more than 200 hits, and in each he's also been named best fielder at his position.

But honestly, the award I was happiest for was another Yankee's. Mark Teixeira won the Gold one as the best fielding first baseman in the American League. I thought I was the only one who noticed all season. Of course, I probably saw him in at least 100 more games than I saw any other first baseman, but if there was someone better than Mark at playing first base, I would have been very, very surprised.

New York recently has a history of great fielding first basemen: Mattingly won Gold Gloves 9 times for the Yankees and Keith Hernandez won 11 Gold mittens (sportswriter talk) for the Cardinals and the Mets. But honestly, after watching Teixeira this season, I'd put him above either of them.

t.

Gilbert AZ – 15 Nov 2009

Dear Terry,

I hate that baseball is over. When the World Series ended Kathy and I were sad that it didn't go all seven games. There were times at night when the house just felt empty, like a tall old creepy house in an H.P. Lovecraft story.

We'd look at the TV screen with nothing on it. I'd say, with morbid gallows humor to Kathy, "is the World Series on tonight?" and she would sadly say no. We both knew it was over.

But there's always *news* of baseball. Always.

Today I read in the paper something that cheered me up and made me laugh wildly. I howled!   It was a story about the athletic director of the University of Texas at El Paso, UTEP. He was talking about how hard it was to recruit baseball players to play college ball at UTEP because the Mexican city of Juarez was right across the border. Right there on the other side of that river.

And, because of the drug wars, over 1,000 murders have happened in Juarez this year alone. One thousand murders. In little Juarez, where college kids like to go play. Here's what was funny in the story. The UTEP athletic director said that he was always honest with the parents of recruits. He acknowledged the problem of Juarez up front. But, he said, but, but, but! "There's no reason to over-exaggerate the problem."

I howled. I mean, he was right! We aren't saying that there are *millions* of murders in Juarez each year. Let us not even suggest that millions have died there. There are *thousands* dead, yes, but *that's it*! Let's not exaggerate it.

(Parents still, the article said, don't want their kids to play ball there.)

I'm starting my autobiography this week.

This is a funny exercise for someone (me) who doesn't want to be remembered. Someone asked me on a radio show once how I wanted to be remembered and I said, "I don't. By anyone. For anything. Why would I want to be remembered? Have people carry the weight of memories of me when their minds could be free and clear to live their own lives?"

I never got asked back on that show.

But after you suggested it to me a couple times and gave me the book *Starbucks Changed My Life* book as an example of what kind of light bio I might write, I saw that it could be pure humor and fun. Which my life has obviously been. That plus a lot of bizarre stuff. You have convinced me to write my bio. My only rule for myself is that it must *only* be funny. (Like Alexander King's was.) If there's a moment in there in which I am seen to take my life seriously it MUST BE REMOVED, and I must consider medication.

(You'll be in the book a lot.)

Sorry this is over. See you in the spring. Maybe we can catch a game. So, anyway ... May this house be safe from tigers,

S

24 Nov 2009 – San Miguel de Allende, MX.

Steve,

Yes, I guess I have to admit the season's over and wrap this thing up. I hate to do it though.

I look back to the beginning of this correspondence, noting with satisfaction that in the very second sentence of my first letter I predicted that the Yankees would win the World Series this year.

I should probably have quit while I was ahead.

After that I predicted that Yankee starters Sabathia, Pettitte, Burnett, Chamberlain and Wang would all win 20 games. None did. Sabathia came closest, missing by only one. Wang, on the other hand, missed by 19!

Later I predicted that Halladay, Grienke and Santana would all win 20. None did.

And finally, with less than a month to go in the season, I predicted that the Cardinals' Adam Wainwright would be the only pitcher to win 20. He didn't.

Maybe I was so bad at predicting 20-game winners because not a *single* pitcher in either the American or National Leagues won 20 this year. The game has changed since our youth; I don't know if you've noticed.

The American League MVP?

I wrote about my hopes for Teixeira and Jeter, but in the end they finished 2nd and 3rd to the Twins catcher Joe Mauer. No problem with that selection, Mauer had a great season. Besides, Teixeira and Jeter got the award that matters – the World Series championship.

I suppose it would be cheating to keep writing baseball stuff when there aren't any more games, huh? Oh well … May this house be safe from tygers,

t.

About the Authors

Steve Chandler and Terrence N. Hill have been writers all their lives. This book is the third in a series that began with the critically acclaimed *Two Guys Read Moby Dick*, followed by the popular *Two Guys Read the Obituaries* and *Two Guys Read Jane Austen.*

Chandler has written and co-written over a dozen books, including the bestseller, *Fearless*. He is a professional business coach and corporate trainer whose previous books have been translated into over 20 languages. His blog, iMindShift, is popular around the world, and you can subscribe at his website, www.stevechandler.com. He lives with his musical wife and editor Kathy and good dog Jim on the scenic outskirts of Phoenix in an old house overlooking Vista Allegre Park.

Terrence Hill worked for more than 30 years in advertising beginning as a copywriter and later running agencies in New York and Europe. He has published poetry, essays and short fiction and was the writer for two CBC-TV (Canada) documentary series. In 2005, Terry's play, *Hamlet-The Sequel,* won the Playhouse on the Green (Bridgeport, Connecticut) playwriting competition. You can email Terry at terrynhill@hotmail.com.

Also by Steve Chandler

RelationShift (with Michael Bassoff)

100 Ways to Motivate Yourself

Reinventing Yourself

17 Lies That Are Holding You Back

50 Ways to Create Great Relationships

100 Ways to Create Wealth (with Sam Beckford)

The Small Business Millionaire (with Sam Beckford)

9 Lies that are Holding Your Business Back (with Sam Beckford)

Business Coaching (with Sam Beckford)

How to Get Clients

Two Guys Read Moby Dick (with Terrence N. Hill)

Two Guys Read the Obituaries (with Terrence N. Hill)

Two Guys Read Jane Austen (with Terrence N. Hill)

Two Guys Read the Box Scores (with Terrence N. Hill)

Business Coaching (with Sam Beckford)

The Hands Off Manager (with Duane Black)

The Story of You

100 Ways to Motivate Others (with Scott Richardson)

10 Commitments to Your Success

The Joy of Selling

Fearless

Shift Your Mind: Shift the World

The Woman Who Attracted Money